The Four Industrial Revolutions

Demystifying Technological Innovation

Tobias Becker

The Four Industrial Revolutions

Demystifying Technological Innovation

Edited by Jocelyn Striker Lemmilä

Cover designed by Tobias Becker

Tobias Becker

Visit my website at www.challenges4.biz

Printed in the United States of America

First Printing: December 2019

Amazon Inc.

ISBN 978-3-00-064551-8

About the Author

Tobias Becker is a 25-year management veteran in the world of engineering and financial services. As a visionary executive dealing with industries as diverse as energy, manufacturing, marine, minerals, and data centers, he had the privilege of performing at the forefront of innovation. He worked on six continents and lived in seven countries. Being an accomplished strategist, operator, and corporate diplomat, he likes understanding business models and organizational design. Tobias is a distinguished speaker who enjoys captivating and engaging audiences, as much as sparring with other thought-leaders on stage. Tobias enjoys sharing insights and experience and dedicates part of his time to lecturing and executive education.

CONTENTS

Foreword

The Fourth Industrial Revolution has become more than an academic thinking construct; it is a societal phenomenon. The sheer phrase strikes fear into the hearts of policy makers and philosophers, of works councils and worried journalists. It is not new that a groundbreaking innovation creates an atmosphere of uncertainty. Great innovations have the ability to be the cog in the machine of paradigm shift and paradigm shifts are among the most challenging situations we humans go through. These shifts are often the most rewarding and even essential. Innovation, though, rarely happens in a vacuum or as an end in itself. Innovation might be a result of some enablers or a confluence of factors, but it is ultimately mostly a solution to a real world problem.

The Four Industrial Revolutions

What we call a revolution is often a loosely connected set of happenings that are only labeled in the aftermath but are a frightening turning point at the time they occur. On the other hand, with the benefit of hindsight, these moments are less frightening, and thus feel less revolutionary. Hindsight allows us to gauge the true effects of such a revolution: the way the revolution solved a burning issue, changed the ability of our species to survive, or formed the basis of a new era. It is an interesting paradox that mankind has seen technical progress lose its shocking properties again and again and become a mainstay and enabler of positive developments, but still the next wave of technical progress will be greeted with the same apprehension. Or perhaps it is purposefully cautious to look at progress in this way?

Let us analyze the areas in which technical innovation happens. I call them the Realms of Innovation and I assert that there are only four of them. I propose that revolutions are merely the latest - and thus still frightening - round of innovation within the four realms. I would like us to go back in time, to the beginning of the each of the Four Realms and work our way forward towards Digitalization, the core of the Fourth Industrial Revolution.

Finally, we will dare to look forward in time beyond Digitalization at what might come next.

CHAPTER ONE

Return on Innovation

The human species is different from the rest of creation, in that we have a relentless drive to invent, to innovate. But this is not an end in itself. Innovation happens when we are confronted with a very real problem. The more essential the problem, the more individuals start working on it, the more of our resources we are willing to sacrifice in the attempt to find a solution. Yes, it is correct that spare time is needed to be creative. But it does not mean that just because it is spare time that this time does not have a value. Creativity and innovation-oriented effort still need to generate payback. An initial idea might be sheer coincidence, but the resulting trials, proof of concept, evolution, and prototyping are based on a conscious investment decision. The opportunity cost would simply be too high. What else could we do with our time, our resources instead? Even doing nothing and just resting can be quite compelling.

In this book, we are discussing the four Realms of Technology Innovation. We claim that all technological progress consists of innovations or improvement of elements within just those four realms, often by combining elements across the boundaries of those realms. We further claim that the latest industrial revolutions are merely the most recent rounds of innovation waves in the very same four realms. What looks revolutionary today will just be a chapter in the progress of mankind when we look back at it a few hundred years from now. By the same token, what we take for granted today was revolutionary at its time. That may have been a century ago, a millennium ago, or even a million years ago. Just imagine the impact the first spear made or the invention of scripts.

Innovation as problem solver

So if innovation is an investment and its actors – us human beings – expect a positive payback, why are we often anxious about innovation? Take the Fourth Industrial Revolution (4IR). The term itself seems to instill fear, seems to conjure up doomsday scenarios. Well, it is not completely surprising. Firstly, people ask themselves what the first three revolutions were. With the count already at four, a pang of having missed out on something important is felt. Did we miss out on the first three? Can we even master the fourth without being maestros of the others? And then, the term 'industrial'. Doesn't it sound daunting, large scale, towering? The term reeks of side effects, pollution, and the common man losing control. And finally, 'revolution' does not exactly create a cozy feeling of certainty, unless you are an anarchist. No wonder most stakeholder groups feel uneasy. Additionally, as we will see a bit later, 4IR is more abstract than many other waves of innovation, more difficult to grasp.

Innovation is tough; it takes resources and much more effort than comprehending it only in hindsight. Whoever is not involved in the creative process, or does not have a license to use a patented idea, feels left out and fears falling

3

behind. People often tend to highlight drawbacks or potential risks. Innovations are often attacked by those who see them as a threat to their livelihood. Take the umbrella. A lightweight, waterproof, collapsible device, that allows one to walk in the rain without getting too wet. It was invented in China and dates back at least 2'000 years. The rain prone Southern part of China is too hot to wear a coat, so an alternative solution was needed. In Europe umbrellas were uncommon even in Middle Ages. Only in the 17th century, when regular contact to China and India through merchants brought a lot of novelties to France and England, the umbrella started to be an alternative to heavy, rainproof coats. Before, only the much lighter and smaller parasol version was used. According to Atlas Obscura, the first Englishman to publicly use an umbrella was shunned and pelted with trash. Jonas Hanway ignored the criticism and proudly used his protection. The most persistent skeptics and the true ringleaders behind the years-long outrage against using umbrellas were the coach and hansom cab drivers, who had especially good business when it rained. They feared that this product was a threat to their income stream. It took five decades for the umbrella to take root in England.

Coming back to the notion of risk. We should not ignore the usefulness of technological impact assessments. Some innovations add more problems than solutions to our civilization, and some are outright counter-productive. But the basic mechanism of innovation is tuned to this sequence: problem, pain, contemplation, and solution. Innovations don't usually just pop up. There is typically a burning platform and people say for a while "wouldn't it be great to have a solution for this". This is the magnet that attracts creativity to a particular problem. Nevertheless, consumers often do not know what a 'good' innovation would be. Asking consumers or users what their ideas are rarely leads to innovation. Ask them what their problems are and how those generate pain. That is the starting point for the creative process of innovation.

But to understand where and when it all started, let me take you back about 2.3 million years in time, a period we refer to as Early Stone Age. Our ancestors are called Homo habilis, or the skillful human.

CHAPTER TWO

The First Realm

I n casual discussions, we often call early human societies the 'hunters & gatherers'. But to be more precise, if at all, we should say 'gatherers & hunters'. We started as gatherers, leaf eaters or folivores and added some tougher foods here and there, like nuts and roots. But mainly our diet was based on fruits and leaves. Our already quite developed brain allowed us to broaden the diet and be rather flexible, understanding where and when to find particular culinary treats. The environment was not too harsh, providing year-round nutrition for the small groups of gatherers living in akin social groups to spread out. Life was not one of hardship. Paleoanthropologists believe that we did not spend more than two to three hours a day with work, though part of that was rather snacking than struggling. So much for the myth that we work less and less in modern times. But let me come back to that a bit later when we discuss another phase.

Success can have implications, and that is what happened to Homo habilis as well. Having so much spare time led to a lot of social interaction, which certainly impacted the progress of the species in the long term. In the short term, it led to proliferation. We became a victim of our own ability to spread, survive, and thrive. With a plant-based diet and the perimeter of activity rather small, the capacity of our environment to sustain the ever-growing population was soon depleted. Our ancestors looked around and saw other mammal species utilizing additional sources of mainly fat and protein. Compared to our herbivorous existence, these predators, and even more so omnivores like bears and wild boar, had huge advantages. But we humans were not made as predators or hunters. Look at our teeth or claws. Rather pathetic. We were not especially strong or fast, nor could we fly or dive. Compare us to the amazing capabilities of the sea eagle, soaring in the air, screening the waters with proverbial eagle eyes, and then darting down with amazing speed and grabbing a fish out of the water. Or a lion striking down an antelope with one mighty blow of its giant paw.

To be able to run as fast as a cheetah or to fly like a hummingbird, the ability to unfold force relative to its weight needs to be pretty high. Our force to weight ratio was not helping. Our force was rather limited. So was our ability to reach. Our physical limitations made it difficult to hunt and kill prey. What sounds like a mere nuisance in today's times of fully stacked fridges was indeed an essential problem, with consequences that could have wiped out our entire species. Starvation would have been a limiting factor for our species to spread out, and in difficult times, due to weather fluctuations or natural disasters, it could have had extinction-level implications. Our forefathers had to do something about it. And they did, unlike several related branches of the Hominina, a meta group of human-like species. Of the Hominina only the group of Australopithecine developed further. And within that group, all species Homo (humans), without exception, became extinct mainly during a time frame between 2.5 and 2 million years ago. After these pivotal 500'000 years only the Homo species was left, which, through several steps, developed into Homo sapiens - the 'wise human'. All herbivore species within the superfamily of Hominina were gone.

Mechanization

Our ancestors observed the strategies of predators in their surroundings. They began to understand the basic principles. The talons of a bird of prey were able to penetrate the fur or armor of its prey. The long beak of a heron, when accelerated suddenly towards its often aquatic prey, allowed fast and deadly reach.

Since these genetically defined properties were missing in our bodies, we needed to augment our bodies. In the most basic form that could mean the use of an existing implement, for example, a branch lying on the ground, or a scavenged antler. We are not alone in this behavior. There are bird species that pick up pine needles and use them as sticky poker to catch ants in their subterranean nests. Others, like the Woodpecker Finch, even break off spines from cactus plants and use these to impale juicy insects that are hiding in the bark of trees, out of the finch's beak reach. So, perhaps copying this behavior, we picked up pointed objects and augmented our body with the early form of a mechanical device. (Or perhaps the birds copied us? We will maybe never know). The principle is rather simple, and we find it in the more sophisticated tools, implements, and weapons such as

9

needles, nails, stitching awls, daggers, and spears. Stitching awls and bone needles were used to puncture sturdy materials, such as bark, wood, fur (or much later leather). This, in turn, allowed further refinement steps, like stitching pieces together to design simple clothing.

The basic mechanical principle is that of amplifying pressure. Pressure is in a physical sense a force F that is applied perpendicularly onto a contact surface A. In the example of the stitching awl, the contact surface is quite small, but a human can easily apply a force equivalent to say 20 kg[1] onto the much larger hilt of the awl. The counterpressure onto the hand is around 0.02 kg/square millimeter, while the pressure at the tip of the awl - let us say the tip is 1 square millimeter - would reach 20 kg per square millimeter, or 1'000 times as much. That is an enormous augmentation of the effect of force. This fur punching, hide perforating, armor-piercing effect is applied in daggers, arrows, spears, and many tools.

Additionally, the tip itself can be shaped. Instead of a blunt one square millimeter stump, the tip can be sharpened into a fine point. Our ancestors did that by using sandstone as a grinder, and later, of course, flint stone blades on softer

---

1 The force would be that in Newton, what 20 kg mass would exert given gravitation on earth.

materials, such as wood or bone. Such a cone-shaped tip, or in the case of a blade, a very sharp wedge, use another mechanical principle in addition to the pressure amplification. The principle is that of the ramp or inclined plane. When moving a burden up a ramp, the incline leads to a longer path during which a steady force can be applied, which in turn can be lower than the force that would be necessary to simply lift an object. This difference in necessary force depends – in this case – on the slope of the incline. The flatter the slope, the bigger the effect. We call this the mechanical advantage of the mechanism. And it leads to a force amplification. Both principles are related, and both belong to the innovation realm of Mechanization.

The Dawn of Skills

As mentioned above, other species are using simple tools. But that is the point; they use readily existing objects. They don't refine them further, and they don't recombine them into composite machines. This kind of purposeful innovation seems to be part of the essence of humanity. Mechanization, or the First Realm of Innovation, opened the gates to a new world: a world of skills. When our ancestors realized that splitting a flint stone with another hard rock generated shards, they also started to understand that the properties of these shards depended on several factors. Which kind of rocks were selected and how were those rocks fixed in position? In which angle was a blow with the 'hammer' delivered, with how much force? Learning about the intricacies of making a stone shard helped to make these components better, to be faster at it, and to improve yield rates. In other words, to be skillful at it. Mechanization led to the dawn of something even more powerful: the Dawn of Skills.

Mechanization and especially its force augmenting effects democratized force. Before, only the strongest specimens in a tribe had a chance to lead, survive, and breed. Leadership, and with it access to food, prime sleeping spots, and sex, was tightly coupled to personal, physical strength. All of a sudden a weaker, but mechanically augmented, and skillful member of a group could challenge that. This moment is so deeply rooted in our human consciousness that is had been subject to myriads of tales and sagas. David versus Goliath, for example, portrays the inferior underdog winning against the powerful brute by using a simple weapon. Though only a simple weapon, the sling, it is a couple of steps further developed than a simple spear. It is believed that the whole idea of detaching weapon and ammunition is a lot younger than the early weapons. Most likely only during the New Stone Age, about 12'000 to 6'000 years ago, humans understood the advantage of protecting the key asset, the weapon. The major difference is that the skill, time, effort, and noble material is invested in producing the weapon, which is retained in the combatant's hands. While only the stone, the ammunition, is depleted. The stone is far less valuable. Compared to using a spear as a ranged weapon, this is a lot more economic. We will see, how the economy has been a driving factor in humanity's efforts for innovation.

Results and further rounds of innovation

To summarize, Mechanization, the First Realm of Innovation:

- Tackled the risk of species extinction from starvation.
- Democratized force, by augmenting our human body with mechanical components that amplify our force.

13

- Kicked off the Dawn of Skills.

Skills made it reasonable to specialize. For the first time, members of a tribe, or even within a family group, could focus on something they were better at than others. This concentration of effort further accelerated the process of skilling up, leading to faster innovation. You could even say the whole business model changed. The way resources were used, especially human resources, changed - in the beginning perhaps gradually, but eventually dramatically. Leading over time to whole societies being structured along the lines of skills. But the solutions that Mechanization created also changed culture and values. The most obvious change was the switch from an herbivore to an omnivore diet. That was indeed the cardinal change that led to the survival of our species. The democratization of force and the Dawn of Skills unleashed humanity's genetic evolution. While before physical attributes completely dominated the selection process, soon skillfulness and mental capacity became equally important. The skills and specialization of individuals in combination with the expanded focus of evolutionary forces within the entire species drastically propelled innovation.

Results and further rounds of innovation

The Realm of Innovation is not a single event. It is a conceptual platform for innovation, based on a particular natural phenomenon. It, therefore, helps mankind to innovate round after round. What we see as revolution is simply the latest groundbreaking round of innovation within a particular realm.

In Mechanization, many rounds of innovation followed. Each one game-changing at its time and each built on top of existing technologies: the wheel, the drill, the needle with an eye, the blowpipe, and eventually compound machines, such as the pulley. Compound machines recombine different simple machines or mechanical components into a complex solution. Take a bicycle. It uses many components and mechanical principles in a rather complex solution. There are two wheels to ride on, but also wheels combined into a pulley to transmit the force from the rider's legs to the wheels of the vehicle. The handlebars make use of levers, so do the brake handles. There are of course loads of screws to hold it all together. Screws are inclined planes, wrapped around a pivot. Even the brake cables stem from one of the groundbreaking waves of mechanical innovation when the principle of the rope got invented. Twisting fibers into yarn, yarn into strands, and strands into ropes create a material that has far more tensile strength than say an equally sized strip of leather. The oldest preserved traces of rope are at least 28'000 years old. Though so far, we only found the indentations of those ropes on clay objects, while the original ropes themselves decayed.

Whole industries were built on the waves of innovations that happened in the First Realm throughout millennia. Once the shackle of force limitation was thrown off, our evolution and technology progress picked up speed. It is important to understand that this development never stopped and most likely never will. Other realms superimpose it over time, and the combination of different realms of innovation has often brought about the most powerful and groundbreaking inventions. But let us see what happened next.

CHAPTER THREE

The Second Realm

The imminent danger of starvation due to overpopulation of the small tribal groups of the immediate surrounding was put in check. With the new omnivore diet and augmented force, the early Homo habilis drove ahead with step-by-step improvements of available technology. Around a million years later, tools had become more sophisticated and carrying both tools and weapons around was likely commonplace. Our species, we now call it Homo erectus, had changed behavior and with it the whole habitus of humans had changed. Only the legs were now used for locomotion, the hands had changed over time, from generation to generation. They no longer served as the second pair of feet, with occasional use for tinkering and instead became more and more dexterous. This upright posture is the namesake of the species at that time. Erectus means upright.

There were threats present in the habitat - predators, but also other groups of humans. The use of hunting weapons for self-defense must have become a part of the behavior of these early humans. The process of collecting food itself was not overly dangerous though. The gathering happened not too far away from the settlements, while hunting was conducted in a bit wider circle, always within a day's walk. Prey was smaller and less powerful than the humanoid hunters themselves. Only accidental collisions with other predators - humanoid or animal - could lead to dangerous conflict.

The skills, with their intrinsic need to source materials, the intimate knowledge of hunting grounds, and also the beginning of accumulating possessions, made static settlements a good idea. While the early Homo habilis moved around in a nomadic fashion, the Homo erectus bands benefited more from staying put and knowing their surroundings well. Over another 500'000 years, their sociality developed further. Taking care of the infirm or weak and burying their dead became a part of the culture of these gatherer and hunter bands.

However, eventually these surroundings started to change. We live today in a geological period called Quaternary. It is a long era of changes between cool periods and warm periods, with colder periods lasting around 100'000 years and warmer periods around 10'000 years. It started coincidentally when our story of human innovation started, more than 2 million years ago. In the middle of what is called the Pleistocene part of it, the temperatures started to drop to an extraordinary low. They were around 15 degrees centigrade lower than before and after. This had some effects on the environment. In some regions, glaciation reduced the available space for living or changed the ecosystems dramatically. Especially in the Northern hemisphere, glaciers covered substantial parts of the land, encroaching both from the North Pole area southward and from mountain ranges into lower valleys. Overall the depressed temperatures presented a challenge to the warm-blooded fauna. To keep the body temperature up, more energy was needed. In a shrinking and less feed-yielding environment, that became a problem. Some species evolved very large bodies. This so-called giantism or megafauna made sense, because the ability to generate body warmth through metabolism grows to the power of three with body size, while the body surface, which loses body warmth in spite of insulation, only grows to the power of two. As a result of this strategy, the large representatives of typical ice age animals came into existence. The Wholly Mammoth developed about 400'000 years ago and was accompanied by other very large animals, both plant-eaters and predators. For our human ancestors, this strategy would not have made as much sense. Our large brain needed a lot of energy and our advantages in terms of skills and technology could have become devalued. Instead the threat of freezing to death needed to be tackled in another way. We needed to find a way to generate warmth beyond the boundaries of our bodies.

Energization

Already during the advent of skills and Mechanization, humans had learned to hunt and make use of practically every part of the prey. The furs were cut into shape and scraped with stone knives, punctured with bone needles, and sewn together with fibers or tendons. This extra insulation layer helped to survive normal winters. Do not imagine such fur to be cozy and pliant. Modern fur is treated and refined. The fur in this period was stiff and smelly. At least it double-served as armor, due to its sturdiness. By the way, the ability to transform fur into leather came much later. That took a new kind of knowledge in another Realm and we will discuss it in a bit. But for now, around 115'000 years ago, the winters were getting longer and colder and solutions for the survival of the species were once again needed, urgently.

Already for some time, our ancestors had observed a phenomenon that was both frightening and intriguing: fire. These combustion processes started frequently due to natural causes, such as lightning strikes or in relevant areas through volcanic activities. Homo erectus lived in areas with both. Especially on the African continent, the origin of the species, bush fires were quite common and they frightened all animal life and humans. A bush fire progresses relentlessly, eating itself through the summer dry Savanna and feeding on the carbon stored in grass, brushwork, and trees. Fanned by winds, a bush fire spreads into a crescent-shaped front, moving in the direction of the predominant wind. While plants fall prey to the flames - and often have developed evolutionary strategies to survive it - animals have to flee. For our semi-settled ancestors, this was not an ideal scenario. It was difficult to haul all their possessions. Leaving the quarries and other material sources behind was crippling. And moving into unknown hunting grounds, which were likely claimed by other tribes, was dangerous. No wonder some groups tried to ride out the firestorm, perhaps in sheltering caves, in rock escarpments or swampy areas. No doubt they then observed something interesting; the fire only consumed organic matter. Well, they might not have had the concept of organic vs. inorganic, but they did realize that water, rocks, and sand were still there. They might also have realized that clay changed its properties from moist, soft, and pliable to dry, hard, and crusty. They must have paid attention to the enormous concentration of prey right in front of the conflagration. I have seen a wildfire in the savanna of Tanzania. Standing right at the edge of the progressing fire you see waves of birds leading the escape, followed by larger mammals, then smaller mammals and especially rodents, and finally grasshoppers, bugs, and other insects. The latter are just staying ahead of the fire front. The fire does not move fast like in the forest fire events in Mediterranean, semi-arid, forested regions. Those fires find much more fuel and the firestorms fan intrinsic winds, sucking in extra oxygen, generating temperatures that make the water in tree trunks expand so fast that even large trees explode. Such fast fires can spread 15 square kilometers per hour. Escaping them becomes almost impossible. A savanna fire moves slowly. Our ancestors became more daring, observed the effects, and made use of the rich buffet of fleeing game. And eventually tried to consume meat from burned animals. Traces of cooked meat consumption go back up to one million years. In the Wonderwerk Cave in South Africa's Northern Cape Province, we find evidence that is around one million years old and the contextual scenario indicates that there was human intervention involved in depositing the cooked food there. There are even older finds in Africa, but they lack this evidence and skeptics believe in natural occurrence.

While Homo erectus might have managed the natural fear and flight reflex and made some conscious use of the phenomenon of fire, it took a much stronger impulse to learn how to master the fire itself. To learn how to control, keep alive, rekindle, or even spark a new fire.

Fire

When temperatures dropped more and more around 120 to 130'000 years ago, our ancestors grasped the importance of controlling fire and managing it, but importantly not yet how to invoke it. They understood that it was based on a process of transforming a fuel, like grass or wood, and that a constant supply of that fuel was needed to keep it going. They understood that some materials burned fast and bright, and others slow and with a glow. They must have tried to burn all kinds of things, experimenting and observing the effects. Was something useful as fuel? Did a material change in nature and properties when it was exposed to the fire? What was useful to extinguish a fire?

Fire and being able to control it was again a solution that ensured the survival of the species. While numerous other uses of fire were complementary and helpful, the one use that was essential was the creation of heat, the ability to transform fuel into warmth. Fuel contains energy that is chemically stored. In most fuels, carbon is at the center of the chemical compound that stores the energy. So-called hydrocarbons are built by plants to store a reservoir of energy gained through photosynthesis. While the sun only shines during the day, and much less so during winter, plants can capture surplus energy and store it. Variations of hydrocarbons are also used to build the structure of the plant itself. Fire transforms the chemical energy in the fuel, through an exothermic reaction, into heat and radiation. Exothermic means that the reaction produces more heat than

24

it consumes, and the fact that this oxidation process is fast means the heat becomes significant. The rusting of iron is an oxidation process as well, and it is exothermic but so slow that in daily life it does not matter. Heat is energy that is transferred to a body and makes its molecules move faster. While they do that they give off radiation, most of it in the form of infrared light, which is invisible to humans but can interact with our tissue and warm us up. The combustion of wood also generates light. Light is visible radiation in a part of the radiation spectrum that our eyes are specialized in detecting.

Fire gave us warmth to survive the ice age. But it also gave us light, expanding our productive days into the evening and nights. It allowed us to deepen our activities in the First Realm and to hone our skills in Mechanization even faster. It helped to conquer shelters that were before off-limits due to complete darkness, such as deep caves and tunnels. It extended the shelf life of food by allowing cooking, smoking, and drying. It also again helped to widen our diet by helping to soften very tough foods. It especially made staple foods available that, without treatment, were poisonous such as potatoes and certain starch-containing tubers, beans, and mushrooms. It even increased nutritional content in food that can be eaten raw, but is far more valuable when cooked, such as corn, carrots, and nightshades like eggplants, tomatoes, peppers and many more.

And of course, the fire kept predators at bay. Mastering fire, the beginning of the Second Realm of Innovation, finally set us completely apart from all other species. While there is some tool use - even if it is more limited - in the animal kingdom when it comes to mastering fire, we are unique. We are the only species that has found a way to systematically manage energy conversion outside of the body. In other words, we learned to throw off the shackle of energy limitations. We are able to add external energy conversion to our metabolic conversion. Like Mechanization overcame the limitation of force, Energization meant prevailing over the limitation of energy.

By the way, in physics, energy is defined as force multiplied by distance divided by time. One could say, the Second Realm contains a bit of the First Realm, and both are connected in the world of physics.

The Dawn of Science

Energization allowed mankind to survive and rise above other parts of creation, in terms of creativity. But the most important side effect was that humans started to understand that their surroundings could be changed, actively. That the properties of materials could be influenced and modified. That for example cooking certain food could make it more filling or better tasting. That drying meat could make it less perishable. That heating certain natural products like tar could change their state of matter, from solid to liquid. That some processes could be reversed. Water freezing to ice could melt back into water. While wood burned to ash would never change back. Building upon the foundation of the skills from the First Realm, the Second Realm brought with it the need and the advantage of experimenting with matter. Testing out what will happen and whether it will improve the results of a process. It meant collecting knowledge about such experiments and their outcomes. Such an endeavor – to actively experiment and collect knowledge – is what we call science. The Latin word 'Scientia' means knowledge. It seems that the first science we humans dealt with was chemistry.

Energization, with its first and most revolutionary outcome, the control over combustion processes, was nothing less than the Dawn of Science. Historians often define the beginnings of science at around 2'000 to 2'500 BCE, with the early cultures in Mesopotamia. And in fact, these civilizations left behind huge amounts of evidence, including writings. The Mesopotamians mastered some processes that were already quite complex applications of chemical processes, for example, the production of soap.

But it started with mastering fire and observing its effects on matter. Clay exposed to heat changed its properties and already around 30'000 BCE humans were able to collect the right kind of clay, shape it into earthenware, and fire it in pits, to create vessels or art objects. The knowledge was passed on, but in the absence of scripts, it was of course not written down. At any rate, at the end of the last Ice Age, around 13'000 years ago, humans had learned how to use fire for a variety of purposes and possessed a compendium of processing know-how for preparing food, making pottery, producing glue, and waterproofing of fibers. They also added new kinds of fuel beyond plant-based carbons. For example, animal fat, which, liquefied to oil, could produce light. These early pottery based oil lamps were much more convenient, long-lasting, and less dangerous than torches made from wood. Mankind would never stop improving ways to shed light.

Hybrid applications

To summarize, Energization, the Second Realm of Innovation:

- Prevented the extinction of our species from freezing.
- Democratized energy, by making it possible to convert and store energy outside of our bodies.
- Kicked off the Dawn of Science.

Science, the collection of knowledge, was also a powerful, game-changing augmentation of our behavior-based capabilities. While the latter was mostly genetic, knowledge needed to be acquired by each individual, over and over again, and be handed down from generation to generation. The teaching of skills was for sure possible with symbolic gestures and by simply demonstrating the work technique. But science made it necessary to enrich the demonstration with some explanations. Words were needed. Language developed. Science was likely a huge motivator to develop proto-language. Before, only sounds were used, for example, to coordinate the attack of a band of hunters on a mammoth.

These sounds were merely acoustic gestures. Around 100'000 years ago, humans started to modify sounds, to compose them into words, and to attach those to objects. Science laid the foundation for the need for languages, and thus later on for scripts.

Throughout millennia, Energization went through many waves. New fuels were detected, such as whale oil, coal, mineral oil, and natural gas. We learned how to raise the energy density in fuels by transforming wood into charcoal in kilns. This allowed reaching higher temperatures needed for smelting metals such as bronze. Black coal laid the base for the iron and steel industries, especially after the coking process for coal was invented which was again a way to improve the fuel in terms of energy density and reduction of impurities.

We learned how to transform the energy in the wind or flowing water into mechanically transmitted kinetic energy. The windmill turning the millstones in a grain mill or pumping water into irrigation systems is a great example. Or take the water wheel driving a transmission belt in a hammer mill. All these variations in capturing energy - transforming, transmitting, or storing it - made industrial activities possible in regions that had before been deprived of those. Another democratizing effect of Energization.

But let me come back to the hammer mill. What a wonderful example of bringing many of the then-contemporary techniques into one great application. The mill was typically situated close to flowing water, for example, a small river or creek, and had a millpond that served as water storage, almost like a battery. The pond often double served as a fire pond for the mill and surrounding businesses and dwellings, not to mention the extra fish farming. The pond also allowed the regulation of the water flow to the water wheel, and a steady pace was maintained by opening and closing a simple flap valve at the start of the so-called mill race. This flume, a kind of man-made channel, brought the water in from the pond upstream, keeping the water level up by putting the flume onto trestles. By this trick, the water flowed down onto the water wheel, accelerated by gravitation and thus having a higher impulse, pushing the blades and thus the entire wheel into rotation. On the other end of the shaft, inside the mill building, a pulley transmitted the rotational energy with a leather-belt onto a belt pulley for distribution of energy throughout the mill. The core process to drive was the large wooden camshaft running low through the forge area. The cams lifted and dropped the hammerheads in a steady rhythm. This hammering emulated the work done by a blacksmith wielding a handheld hammer and forging iron on an anvil. The difference is that the hammers of the mill were much more powerful and were able to strike several times per second. There was no need for an apprentice or blacksmith's striker to help. The smith was fully focused on manipulating the workpiece.

The iron was smelted on the other side of the mill using charcoal to fire up the smith's heart. Large bellows constructed from wood and leather, driven by an eccentric tappet via an auxiliary belt off the main transmission shaft, blew extra air into the fire in preparation of the smelting action. Once the sponge iron or bloom was hot enough and pliable, the worker took the material with a large gripper over to the hammers.

It is important to understand that a lot of the revolutionary potential of innovation comes to fruition when innovations from different realms are blended into hybrid applications of technologies. A hammer mill combines numerous Mechanization and Energization technologies into one composite system. Energy is transformed and transmitted multiple times, from the potential energy of the stored water in the pond, through linear flow, vertical drop, into rotational work, using pulleys, belts, wheels, shafts, and again the transformation into a linear up and down movement. The chemical processes at play are equally astonishing. Wood enriched in charcoal kilns into higher energy density fuel is used to change the state of matter of iron ore from solid to liquid, while introducing carbon material into the mix, creating an alloy. The hammering not only shapes the bloom but also induces enormous heat into the iron lump, keeping it very hot and pliable. It is a perfect example for hybrid applications, mixing inventions from two different realms.

The hydropower driving the wheel was renewable and so was the wood for the charcoal. However, the industry was so successful that it quickly grew and the consumption of charcoal outstripped the regeneration capacity of the surrounding forests. The carbon balance was therefore negative. More trees vanished per year than grew, thus capturing back less carbon. For the first time in history, mankind's carbon footprint became an issue due to the ability to convert energy outside of our bodies.

CHAPTER FOUR

The Third Realm

The ice age had been a tough period, and without technological progress, without Energization and the Second Realm, our species might have stopped being a subject of our planet's history books. But at least the ice age also had some advantages. The reduced space due to glaciation, further reduced habitable areas due to extreme temperatures, the shorter growing seasons, and the concentration of accessible liquid water, forced prey onto more and more confined territories. Plus, the prey got a lot bigger. You could say that a mammoth was the supermarket of prehistoric times. It contained almost everything a tribe needed, in abundance: building materials, raw materials for bone tools and clothing, tendons for sewing, protein, and fat.

It needed coordination, language supported efforts, weapons, and logistics to make use of this opportunity. And for sure a lot of guts.

At the end of the ice age, a period started which we call Holocene. The ice retreated and the temperatures started to rise slowly, and the whole situation changed. The megafauna vanished, giantism was no longer an advantage. The landscape left behind by the retreating glaciers was bleak, with crops and game being spread wide over an ever-growing tundra. The former concentration of prey was replaced with high entropy. Both hunters and gatherers had to invest substantially more time to collect nutrition. During tougher periods, this could lead to a negative net energy gain. In other words, in an attempt to collect enough food, the bands of proto-neolithic hunters were exhausting their energy reserves. They had to cover too long distances and spend too much time away from the settlement only to return with less than enough food. Our species was again facing a major problem. A thousand years after the ice age, temperatures had risen enough, vegetation had changed, and food density recuperated. But how could our species bridge those 1'000 years without succumbing to exhaustion?

36

New methods were needed. We needed to hunt for more than the typical 8-10 hours per day – 16, 24 or even more hours were needed. Impossible! Resting time was important and time was limited to 24 hours a day. We needed to find out how to hunt while sleeping, or how to hunt in several places at the same time. We needed to overcome the limitation of time itself. Throw off its shackles. What was needed was the Third Realm of Innovation. We call this Automation.

Automation

When we hear 'automation' we think of robotics, of large control systems in industrial plants. But what was the first automaton mankind developed? Automation is defined as a machine or mechanism that, once started, follows a predetermined sequence of operations. So obviously a product of the First Realm, in terms of the mechanical structure, but brought to life with Energization from the Second Realm.

Imagine that our Neolithic hunters took a fresh twig or sapling and fixed it to the ground on one side, then bent it and fixed the other end with a little trigger-like contraption. To that end, they affixed a small arrow or dagger. The mechanism is now charged and stores energy resting in the deformation of the bent twig, equal to the amount of force needed to bend it. Once set up, the mechanism rests and, if built smartly, it stays active for a long time. When an animal steps onto the trigger, the energy in the spring (the twig) discharges, driving the arrow into the prey and killing it. These first automata and many variants of it were what we call traps. And traps allowed hunting without being present; to hunt in several - even in dozens - of places at the same time, even while sleeping. The hunting process became detached from the time synchronization needed for conventional hunts. Being at the right spot at the right time was no longer needed. Time itself was circumvented by the trappers. This is the essence of Automation, the Third Realm of Innovation. The shackle of time gets thrown off. In the post-glacial tundras, this boost in productivity came as a lifesaver. The net energy gain from trapping was far superior to that of hunting. This aspect of economic advantage and increased energy efficiency is visible as a red thread throughout the millennia of progress in Automation.

Once the basic principle and its economic advantage were discovered, mankind applied it to numerous fields. Traps were refined and improved. New materials and killing methods applied, such as dropping a stone onto the prey in the case of the deadfall trap. In a trapping pit, the idea is reversed; the prey falls through a camouflaged surface that does not support its weight into the pit, which is constructed to prevent escape. Similarly, fish traps or lobster pots have a way in, but the flexible guards between the entry and the chamber snap shut and do not let the prey out. These traps have the advantage of keeping the prey alive and they can catch several animals. Compared to spring traps and snares, they can be constructed with selectivity in mind. Small fish can escape, or small animals do not trigger the trap at all.

Many rounds followed, each with the potential to be revolutionary at the time. Take the invention of the automatic counter, and then the clock. Or a number of automatic shutdown mechanisms that stopped an operation automatically when completed. A nice example is the level indicators used in old water wheel–driven flour mills. When the barrel capturing the flour falling from the millstones was full, the level lever dislodged the cogwheel driving the millstones, thus stopping the grinding process. This avoided overflow and unnecessary wear on the millstones. When the miller heard the mill stopping, all he had to do was switch to an empty barrel and reset the level indicator, restarting the grinding process. This allowed one miller to operate numerous stations thereby reducing the necessary miller's toll, the portion of flour kept by the miller as payment. The toll reduction meant that the custom mills in the hands of farmers or communities became less and less economic. At the end of the 18th century, merchant mills started to become the norm in all but remote areas. Once this specialization kicked in, it allowed more and more investments within the three Realms. The transport systems within the mill were all mechanized with bucket belts, and the supply of energy improved from hand drives, via animal drives, to water wheels of larger dimensions. And more process steps were automated, improving productivity and energy efficiency, but especially the quality of the end product. In conventional mills, the grain and the flour were manually moved around, spread out for drying, then raked back together. This involved not only a lot of manual labor, but also contaminated the product a lot. The process was not very uniform, leading to fluctuations in the properties of flour. That in turn made it more difficult for bakers to produce a uniform quality of bread. As Oliver Evans, the greatest innovator in the grain mill industry of the time, put it, "people did not even then like to eat dirt if they could see it".

Automation reduced the human input time per unit of production. By the way, we discussed before that energy is force multiplied by distance divided by time. Do you see how the first three Realms of Innovation hang together? They tackle force, energy, and time. The most basic principles of physics.

The Dawn of Education

Automation at the beginning of the Holocene was the savior of our species. Trapping allowed us to multiply the productivity of conventional hunting. But the true extent of what Automation can do for mankind became visible only thousands of years later. At that point in time, manual production in manufactories, mostly inside the homestead of artisans or subsistence farmers, was mainly a complementary income stream. The key resource to keep that business running was spare time. Small merchants used calm periods to hand make some products, or farmers got busy during the quiet winter period. Investments had to be kept to the bare minimum. Only when that changed, at the advent of the First Industrial Revolution when capital was instead the main driver for output, Automation started to be essential for the economics of production.

But first, the hunger for labor force was enormous. The entrepreneurs invested fortunes in production sites, employing the newest technologies of the First and Second

Realm, betting everything on making the right decisions. Those investments had to generate payback so the expensive machines had to be kept running. While during the medieval period and the preindustrial phase weekly work times of 18 to 22 hours were normal (perhaps more during harvest times and less during off-season), the Industrialization period asked for 60 hours or more. Workers, recruited from rural areas, saw a chance to become part of urban opportunities and brought with them the work ethics and physical strength of self-employed farmers. These workers, suddenly working for 60 hours a week, were so exhausted that almost no other activity than working and perhaps a church visit on Sundays was possible. Life became a long and boring stretch of hard and often dirty and dangerous work. Time became the luxury good of the early industrialization. Only the elite had time. Everyone else was stripped of time completely. Schools were not for everybody, and even children who had the chance were often taken out of school at a young age. In the subsistence farmsteads and small artisan workshops, knowledge had been passed down from generation to generation and crafts were trained in the guild system through apprenticeships, but the new breed of factory workers knew nothing except a few tricks and low level semi-skills at best. Industrialization lifted the ability of humankind in terms of know-how on a species level, but the level of know-how of the vast majority of individuals was diminished. Unskilled labor became the raw material of the era.

Only when Automation kicked in and drove productivity up dramatically, this finally changed. Boosts in productivity allowed payment of better wages and gradually reduced daily and weekly work hours. Eventually Saturday became a default part of the weekend and work hours trended towards 40 hours a week. Laborers joined Sunday schools to learn how to read and write. The concept of lifelong learning for the broad masses, or popular education, gained more ground. Although the first folk high schools already opened in Denmark in 1844, it took almost half a century to penetrate most of the former Hanseatic League area in Europe, with Finland, Germany, Switzerland, Austria, Sweden and Norway being early adopters. Broad-based education was enabled by elevated productivity, giving time back to the common man, but it was also needed to operate the more and more sophisticated machines. Unskilled labor was no longer sufficient. Vocational education was needed to match the human skills with the more and more demanding operations of powerful and versatile machines. In some parts of the world, the dual education systems for vocational professions created a new blue-collar elite: highly paid, skilled workers who specialized in hundreds of professions. Some based on old arts, such as the profession of the smith, but many completely new, matching technology progress in the Third Realm. Automation not only gave time back to people and democratized time, allowing even the lower echelons in society time to socialize during the weekend and evenings, and to join clubs and sports activities, but it also fostered the Dawn of Education. Only productive workers and employees have the time to learn, and only skilled personnel have the capabilities to generate payback for highly capital intensive investments in technology.

Once more we summarize. Automation, the Third Realm of Innovation:

- Prevented the extinction of our species from exhaustion.
- Democratized time, by boosting our productivity and reducing the weekly work hours.
- Kicked off the Dawn of Education.

We will look at automation again at a later stage, when we discuss the Third Industrial Revolution.

Waves

We already learned that innovation within a realm never stops. There are many rounds. We also saw that many of the powerful inventions make use of technologies across the boundaries of the innovation realms, forming hybrid solutions. But there are also moments in human development where some key pivotal and complementary innovations occur at roughly the same time. Those amplify each other and fuel each other's success and market penetration. They build up a wave. If such a wave is strong enough, it has the potential to wash away incumbent ways of doing things. All of a sudden, pieces of the puzzle fit together, forming a new way of thinking and enterprising.

Take the early 1950's. In an attempt to improve the process for creating letterpress plates, Oskar Suess and Louis Plambeck Jr. had been working on improving the lithographic process. First Suess's positive photoresist concept and then Plambeck's Dycryl polymeric plate, which improved the speed of making plates, propelled new ideas forward. One example was how to use this photographic process in areas other than printing. The fact that light is a much more precise tool than any mechanical means of etching structures into a print plate opened the opportunity to create very fine structures. Structures much finer than any normal print process even needed.

At the same time, based on the work of Julius Edgar Lilienfeld on field-effect transistors, a group of researchers around William Shockley tried to create a working prototype of such a transistor. This prototype was eventually implemented as a point-contact transistor for which Bardeen, Shockley, and Brattain were awarded the Nobel Prize in Physics in 1956. They managed to master what Lilienfeld had patented but could not yet manufacture: semiconductor devices that can be used to switch or amplify electronic signals. The key was the photolithographic process, which is still the core process in modern semiconductor fabrication plants.

Transistors had so many advantages over the vacuum tube technology that they quickly penetrated most applications where tubes had been used before. Paramount was a concept that for decades would play center stage in electronics: miniaturization. Since the manufacturing process was using light to inscribe structures, more and more instances of transistors could be placed onto one integrated circuit - the so-called chip. The far lower power consumption, ruggedness against mechanical shocks, the absence of glass envelopes, and also the resilience and low wear and tear, were advantages that allowed a huge number of new applications, e.g. portable, battery-powered systems such as pocket radios. No wonder the invention of the alkaline battery falls into the same time frame. These batteries displaced the then typical zinc-carbon batteries because they had far better battery life.

The combination of miniaturized circuits on a transistor base, higher efficiency, and convenient batteries triggered a flood of paradigm changes, from audio and video technology to wristwatches and pocket calculators. A huge wave of progress and innovation had begun, and along with it the starting point of many companies that are still hallmarks of the era such as Intel, Texas Instruments, Seiko and others. This is what we mean by a wave.

CHAPTER FIVE

The Fourth Realm

B ut let us go back in time again. Our Proto-Neolithic ancestors have entered the ice age and found a way to deal with the energy limitation. And they survive. They are more dependent on bands and social structures because the prey they hunt is massive and dangerous. The surroundings are tricky and dominated by harsh weather and adverse climate conditions. But there are periods of relative tranquility. Several tens of thousands of years into the ice age, we are back in control and have mastered the situation. Fire, improved hunting techniques, trapping pits, and the first projectile-based weapons allow us to stabilize the course of our evolution.

When people have time, they socialize and they become creative. Imagine - we learned how to bring light into caves and were able to use them as shelter. We also took advantage of the fact that caves are inside and not subject to weather. Our ancestors used ochre to paint on the walls of caves. They started by using their hands as a stencil, spraying ochre and water mixtures onto the hands and leaving a negative print of the hand on the wall. Leaving a trace of themselves. Soon, more artistic paintings occurred. But let's stay with those simple stencils for a moment. While they might seem inferior to a drawing, they do represent the first example of printing. The idea of using a template to reproduce a symbol will become so much more important over time. Simple templates and symbols become pictograms, hieroglyphs, and characters, and at a certain point the idea is born that symbols could also represent sounds. This gives rise to scripts.

But let us look a bit closer at what cave paintings really are, and what powerful beginning they represent. Since the advent of proto-language around 100'000 ago, humans used words not only to coordinate activities but also to tell stories. In the middle of the last ice age, around 60'000 years ago, oracy, the ability to speak, was sufficiently developed to share stories around the campfire. Elders explained animals and their behavior to youngsters, enriching the story with gestures and imitations of animal movements and sounds. They shared memories of what they had seen or heard. Oracy allowed them to revisit a memory and to relay it to a counterpart. It became a key ingredient of teaching, as part of the Dawn of Education. But the limitation was that both the person sharing a thought and the recipient had to be present at the same time at the same place. At the moment of sharing, information was exchanged but it remained volatile like the smoke of the campfire itself. It only resided in the head of the people. Memories were limited to storage in peoples' minds.

That changed with cave paintings. Memories were preserved on the walls. For the first time in history they existed outside of the human body, outside of the brain. The representations fell short of the precision, dynamics, and colors of the true memories. They didn´t move and were silent, monochrome and rough. But they were stored outside of the brain for others to see. And from that moment on, mankind would never stop refining the quality and resolution of stored imagination or memory. The Fourth Realm of Innovation started with oracy, which expressed a thought, but its greatest breakthrough came with the ability to write the thought onto a wall. The stenciled hand became a pictogram, a symbol. And soon our ancestors added more symbols for a variety of animals, of course, and symbols for people and landmarks. Composing those symbols allowed us to draw simple maps. A map shares an instruction, a short story of how to get from A to B. Before that, a person had to lead another person from A to B, to show the way. Now the knowledge became detached and could be shared with persons not even present at the moment the message was relayed. The stem of the word information comes from Latin and means 'to give form'. The Latin verb 'informare' means to 'give form to the mind'. That is what the Fourth Realm is all about: the Informatization of everything we humans deal with. It started with paintings. For sure a lot of which were made and vanished like a stick drawing in the sand on the beach. Swallowed by the next tide. Those in caves were sometimes preserved. The oldest known cave paintings in Europe are in the cave of El Castillo in Spain and are around 40'000 years old. But our African forefathers were much earlier. The oldest painting ever found so far was found on a rock fragment in the Blombos Cave a couple of hundred kilometers east of Cape Town. The ochre drawing is around 73'000 years old.

Informatization

Informatization started with oracy and the ability to tell a story. Sitting around a campfire, the purest expression of the Second Realm, telling a vivid story and entertaining or educating our family and friends is the essence of the Fourth Realm. With symbols came maps and with abstract representations came scripts. Literacy allowed us to capture a story and write it down, bridging time and overcoming the necessity of the physical presence of the audience. It also provided a way to document an agreement. If you give me A, I will give you B. Simple barter deals were engraved onto a clay tablet and burned to preserve the agreement. Cast in stone, so to speak. That aspect of Informatization got a real boost when we understood the concept of counting. Counting had a lot of uses. Keeping track of days, for example. When a hunting band left the settlement, both the travelers and those waiting at home wanted to know how many days had passed and when the party should return. Tally sticks were used for such purposes; tally marks were cut into wood or bone sticks or a marble was moved every day by one field in a tally roster. This allowed counting the days within the lunar cycle as well. In the simplest form, tally marks were inscribed into a soft material like clay, fat, or simply sand. These tally marks were simple vertical strokes. The first four Roman letters still contain the concept. Counting on fingers might have been the first technique and also served for sign language purposes, for example during deerstalking. Some of the oldest tally sticks, like the Lebombo bone found in the Lebombo Mountains in South Africa, are around 40'000 years old. There are older, decorative uses of markings on bones, around 80'000 years old, but they lack the presumed purpose of counting.

Tallying systems lack the concept of using place value in the notation of numbers. That makes it difficult to represent and comprehend large numbers. Also, arithmetical operations are rather difficult. That is why positional numeral systems quickly displaced the early counting systems. Understanding numbers and getting an intuitive feel for them, as well as developing strategies to perform simple arithmetic, is what we call numeracy. Mathematics has its home in the Fourth Realm.

Informatization was from the start all about codifying knowledge. And many of the great rounds of innovation in its field were about the dissemination of knowledge. Early books were handcrafted, often lavishly decorated, and illuminated with beautiful illustrations in color. They focused on spiritual and religious topics and were often handwritten by monks, which made sense since the ability to write and read was concentrated on the clerical and feudal elite. Books were treasures, produced as a unique copy or in a very small edition. A monk could spend a year to complete an ornate manuscript. Classics from the Hellenic period were also sought after. The demand for books grew with the new middle class of traders and merchants, the so-called bourgeoisie. They could read, were running businesses, and they were accumulating wealth. A library reflected that success. Woodcarvers created blocks with text and monochrome pictures for each page of a book. These woodcuts of the 14th century enabled the printing of an entire book. The storage and handling of the blocks were of course quite demanding. In China, where the woodblock printing originated around 200 CE, it helped to spread Buddhism and the largest project was to print the entire canon of the Tripitaka, the Buddhist scriptures. In the 10th century, a version of the Tripitaka with 130'000 pages was carved and then printed during a 22 years effort. Imagine the amount of wood.

The Dawn of Trade

One of the most powerful applications of numeracy was the idea of assigning value to a token. The early Neolithic humans exchanged gifts of assumed equal value, even without a deal. Gifting, without the guarantee of any return, established debt. In the next stage the late Neolithic era, this debt was defined and described. So the gift and counter gift was clearly agreed and a barter deal established. But barter deals needed both of the parties who possessed the goods to be exchanged to be present in the same physical spot. What if party B did not have what party A wanted, but knew someone who did – party C? Such deals involving three parties needed an intermediate valuable to be carried by party B from A to C to obtain the goods in question and bring them back. The value of the deal had to be symbolized by a token. A token that was true and original. That had intrinsic value, for example, because of the material it was made of. Such a token is called a commodity token. It was nothing other than the first money.

With literacy and numeracy becoming more sophisticated, and the concept of money becoming a key pillar of economic activity, complex contracts could be encoded, signed, and followed up. Commodity tokens were often heavy and cumbersome to store and transport. They also were not protected against theft. Thus, paper-based money – or representative money – was invented. It certified a determined value and, for example in the form of a check, defined who was entitled to receive a certain sum of money from a particular debtor. Such a bill of exchange protected the transaction from theft and allowed trading without carrying a lot of money around.

Once the concept of a value token existed, the concept of price was born. Numeracy allowed us to determine a spot price and also to codify prices and establish a price level. That applied even for barter deals. When fur traders established contact with the First Nations on the North American continent, a variety of barter commodities were accepted such as gunpowder, alcohol, or tobacco. A particular kind of pelt fetched a certain price expressed in gunpowder and another expressed in alcohol.

The true power of Informatization lies in it being the foundation of commerce. The Fourth Realm kicked off the Dawn of Trade.

Entropy

When we think about the Fourth Realm, we see that information is the measure - the basic element - this realm is built on. Like the First Realm is built on force, the second on energy, and the third on time. Those three are related and best expressed in these simple formulas:

Force is defined as $F = \dfrac{m \cdot d}{t^2}$ or mass (m) times distance (d) divided by time (t) to the power of two.

Work is defined in the simplest linear case as $W = F \cdot d$ or Work (W) equals a constant force (F) being applied linearly over a distance (d).

Or, if we replace F with the first formula: $W = \dfrac{m \cdot d \cdot d}{t^2}$

Energy can be seen as the ability to perform work and we measure it in Joule: $J = \dfrac{kg \cdot m^2}{s^2}$, which reflects the above formula for work (W). Here mass is given in kilogram (kg), distance in meters (m), and time in seconds (s). You could as well express this non-metric, for example in horsepower.

Energy, in the form of chemical energy stored in a log of wood, has the ability to perform a certain amount of work, realized for example in the form of heat, if the energy is converted by a fire-induced combustion process.

So we see how the first three realms hang together. But what about the fourth? To understand that, we should quickly look at what our human activity in the three other realms means and what consequences it has. To get a handle on that analysis, we could have a look at the phenomenon of entropy. In layman's terms, entropy could be described as losing a part of the energy in a conversion process to non-useful energy. Imagine a world in which all potential energy was stored in one giant storage container and nothing was happening with it. The entropy of that theoretical system would be zero or very close to it. Or to express it a bit more practically, there would be total order. This situation would be easy to describe with information. Since only one object exists, containing one entirety of all potential energy, one would not need a lot of memory to describe it. Now imagine this potential energy would be released and converted into another form of energy, say pressure. If that would happen in an ideal system, without any losses, the entropy would still be the same, close to zero. But in reality that is not what happens. Any real process has losses - take friction for example. Friction generates heat, which leaves the process and escapes as radiation. The more often energy is converted and the higher the specific losses of such processes are, the higher the change of entropy is of the overall system. You could say that there is more and more disorder. And that disorder would also need more and more information to be described. Just picture the children's playroom after a lively birthday party. If you would like to tell a friend on the phone where everything is in the room, it would take hours. All the toys are scattered around. In physics, we would say there was a lot of dissipation. Dissipated energy, or matter can, in many cases, be put back together. The process is then reversible. But after putting it back together, the entropy is not restored to where it was because the process of putting it back together inevitably leaks energy, and thus losses. It is still worth the effort, since leaving the chaos has higher entropy than investing some losses to restore the original state. Many processes, however, are non-reversible. If the kids during that birthday party dropped a glass of juice onto the carpet, there is a bit of non-reversible entropy. The glass is broken and cannot be put back together. And the juice cannot be taken out of the carpet and collected back into a glass. Most of it has forever dissipated.

Optimization

You might say, however, that the glass didn't always exist. When it was created, some highly scattered materials, such as sand, or in chemical terms silicon dioxide, were connected into a crystalline material and shaped into a particular form. Indeed, we call this negentropy. Negentropy reverses entropy and creates structure, like the crystal matrix of the glass. It is the opposite of entropy. Living things tend to organize scattered materials and build structures out of those. Plants, for example, collect dissipating radiation from the sun and highly scattered CO_2 from the atmosphere, as well as water molecules randomly distributed in the ground, to form higher-level carbohydrates, such as sugar or starch. They can even add some even more complex organic polymers, such as lignin, to form woody structures. The result - say a eucalyptus tree - is a miracle of order, developed out of highly entropic bits and pieces. The same applies when an herbivore, for example, a koala bear, eats the leaves of that tree. The animal again utilizes the components the leaves are made from to build even more complex, higher organized structures, like a variety of tissues, organs, and brain. Living organisms do this all the time and the busier they are, the more heat they produce.

Does that mean life reverses entropy overall? Locally it does. The more life flourishes on our planet, the higher the negentropy and the lower the disorder. However, all of this needs a driving force. The system needs an external feed of energy. This energy arrives on our planet after an eight-minute journey from the Sun. The Sun is a star and runs a constant hydrogen fusion process that fuses an estimated 600 million tons of hydrogen to helium, every second. That is a lot of energy. Fortunately, due to that energy being radiated in all directions, and due to the distance of the Earth from the Sun, only a fraction of that energy arrives on our planet. Scientists calculated that about one-tenth of one billionth of the Sun's energy hits the Earth. This energy is used by plants for photosynthesis, as described above. All other organisms are heterotrophs. That means they cannot produce their food by themselves and have to acquire their food by absorbing organic material from other organisms. That, of course, applies to us humans.

The Sun is by far our largest source of energy, even if we often make use of the Sun's radiation in indirect ways. A hydropower plant uses water from a storage lake to run its turbines. But how did the water get there? It rained down on the mountain range and collected in a river, which feeds the lake. The rain originates from water in large bodies of water dissipating, like oceans, driven by the energy that the Sun radiates into our atmosphere and onto the planet. That means other renewable energy sources, such as biomass, hydropower, and wind are all indirect solar energy. The process of the fusing of hydrogen produces enormous amounts of waste heat on the Sun and is a massive driver of entropy. So, yes, locally on Earth, life generates negentropy, but overall the Sun produces far more entropy. So, even on a universe level, the second law of thermodynamics applies. It says that the total entropy of an isolated system always increases over time. Entropy has a direction coupled with time. Scientists call this often the Arrow of Time.

In the end though, the Sun will burn out, with all fuel consumed, and will slowly cool down until it reaches the ambient temperature of the surrounding space.

We mentioned before the connection between entropy and the amount of information necessary to describe a particular state of entropy. When organisms organize matter into a complex structure, they are reducing their entropy. We do the same, when we build structures, for example, a house. We humans can additionally organize information into something more complex and meaningful. The creation of information works like a vector against dissipation and chaos. Information, made useful in the hands of people, accelerates the formation of physical structures and raises the efficiency with which these structures are being built. A process in the first three realms can be made more efficient with Informatization. Efficiency is a measure of the ratio between yield and waste. Remember? Every conversion of energy or matter creates waste, resulting in entropy. But the more efficient the conversion, the lower the waste. Societies that drive Informatization and foster the democratization of knowledge allow their members to improve efficiency and reduce local entropy. In the chapter on the Fourth Industrial Revolution, we will dissect further how the competitiveness of societies can be defined in relation to their ability to curb entropy with Informatization.

The deepest problem that the Fourth Realm helps us to resolve is the problem of entropy. At the heights of Industrialization, the rate of mankind generating entropy became a staggering threat to our entire existence. We were – and still are - about to overload our planet and reverse the negentropy that biological life had accumulated for billions of years on our fragile planet.

So let us capture another summary. The Fourth Realm of Innovation, Informatization, has the following key effects:

- Prevented the extinction of our species from entropy.
- Democratized knowledge, by capturing, preserving, and disseminating information.
- Kicked off the Dawn of Trade.

We will look at entropy again at a later stage when we discuss the first two Industrial Revolutions.

Overview of the Realms

Below you find an overview of the four Realms of Innovation and their key implications.

Realm of Innovation	Mechanization	Energization	Automation	Informatization
Throws of the shackle of...	Force limitation	Energy limitation	Time limitation	Information storage
Rescues humankind from...	Starvation	Freezing	Exhaustion	Entropy
First key innovation	Knife	Fire	Trap	Cave painting
Democratized...	Physical force	Access to energy	(spare) time	Knowledge
Kicked off the dawn of...	Skills	Science	Education	Trade
Latest revolution	Industrialization	Electrification	Robotization	Digitalization

We can also look at how the four Realms are coexisting and interact with the activity of a human being as an energetic system in the sense of thermodynamics. Any bio-physical system, like a plant, and animal, or a human has a state of internal energy and entropy. Whenever energy is injected into the system, it drives a small increment of entropy. On the other hand, the internal energy level goes up a notch. That means the potential of this individual to perform work grows. All this energy can be made useful for the purpose of life itself. That can mean to move around, to hunt, gather, reproduce, or to think. That is true, unless there is an energy drain. During the Ice Age, the extreme cold was such an energy drain. The illustration below shows how the balance of energy input vs. work output can get disbalanced if the energy loss gets too large. During the Ice Age, humans used the Realm of Energization to counter that loss with energy conversion outside their metabolism. But what happens if there is not enough food?

Then the energy input becomes smaller than the work output. That happened early on to our non-omnivore brothers and sisters, and they became extinct. Our species used Mechanization to add more food and regrow the input vector. After the Ice Age, when energy loss was no longer a problem, there was enough food, but it was quite dispersed. To gather that or hunt for it needed to much work output. Again, the balance got skewed, and Automation allowed us to inject more time by using traps and stabilize the balance, by reducing the necessary work output.

Informatization is what helps us to improve the inner efficiency of our existence and curb the build-up of entropy. The negentropy generated by information and knowledge allows us to get more progress out of the internal energy our system contains.

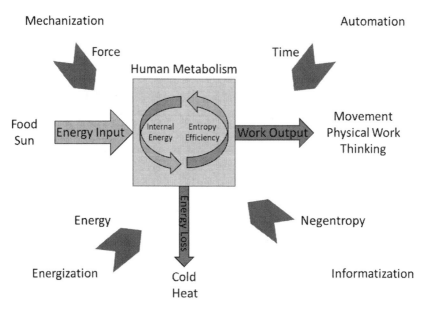

We see how the Realms build upon each other and are woven into an overall physics framework. They all address urgent needs and work in rounds of innovation, again and again. Combinations or hybrid solutions are more likely to be the basis for what we call a wave of innovation. Such waves, in a fertile context, can trigger a revolutionary step change of progress.

In the next chapter, we will have a bit deeper look at the more recent rounds of innovation and the corresponding waves and paradigm changes and at how those led to Industrial Revolutions.

CHAPTER SIX

The first three industrial revolutions

We moved around the eons, touching on the starting points of the Four Realms of Innovation, observing our ancestors leveraging the power of Mechanization, Energization, Automation, and Informatization. In this chapter, we will take a closer look at the recent history and understand how the first three Industrial Revolutions impacted progress and society.

For sure we have skipped over one important aspect of the development of early humanity. While we talked about the addition of hunting to the original gathering base of foraging, and later on the great progress of trapping, there is, of course, a period that brought extremely important change: the introduction of agriculture. Humans started to value wild grains around the time the Third Realm started. Grains and other grasses spread after the end of the Ice Age and the grasslands were the home of several cereal grains. Early Neolithic villages show traces of both tools for cereal processing and cereal residue, which indicates that using grains as sustenance goes back around 100'000 years. When processing grain, villagers understood that wherever they had accidentally dropped a number of collected grains, the density of these useful plants grew. It took quite a while for mankind to fully grasp what it takes to systematically grow a particular type of cereal grain. The earliest traces of systematic planting of fig trees are found in the valley of the Jordan River and date back more than 10'000 years. Domestication of cereals followed a millennium later in Syria, and then other parts of the Fertile Crescent. The so-called founder crops were - amongst others - einkorn wheat, barley, and emmer wheat. These grains were a potent addition to the Neolithic diet. And they were yet another reason to become sedentary.

So, what Realm are we talking here? Agriculture does not augment our force, is not an automatic process, and has nothing to do with coding information. In principle, it is a typical Energization topic. By storing part of the harvest, energy is stored in chemical form instead of being consumed. This self-restriction pays back when, during planting season, the stored grain is invested, grows, and yields a multiple of the original input during harvest. Roughly at the same time as the advent of food crops, fiber crops were also being domesticated. China was focused on hemp, Africa and South America on cotton, while in other parts of Asia flax was important. Agriculture allowed for the first time production of such a surplus of food that an entire part of the population was in a position to step out of subsistence activities and concentrate solely on crafts. Since crafts often benefited from elements of the value chain being co-located, urban centers started to develop. Farms were pushed to the outside of the settlements, while before they were the center of a settlement. The specialization that started with skills a million years before was now transforming entire societies, leading to a stratification of the population into primary and secondary sectors. It is intriguing to note that today we call the Middle Ages the Dark Ages and experience a morbid shudder when thinking about this era. In reality, the High Middle Ages was a relatively peaceful period. The only military activities were the crusades, happening far away from a European point of view. There were no major pandemics. The first universities were founded. Connecting faith and ratio, and improving methods for growing and processing food, allowed a rather homogeneous population to grow significantly.

Agriculture intensified at the end of the Middle Ages. Via Al-Andalus new crops, such as oranges, cotton, and rice were introduced from the Islamic world. After 1492, the exploration of the Americas by Columbus brought a host of new crops, such as maize, potatoes, tomatoes, and sweet potatoes back to Europe. And from there they traveled further through the Islamic world into West Asia and Africa. New methods, like the application of fertilizer, irrigation systems, and crop rotation allowed improved yield rates. This allowed populations to grow significantly, and cities to grow in both size and population density. With the exchange of goods between Asia, the Middle East, Europe, and the Americas, something else was exchanged as well: infectious diseases. The Black Death, a plague, most likely based on the Yersinia Pestis bacterium, originating from the plains of Central Asia, traveled along the Silk Road with merchants, and hit Eurasia with the largest pandemic in human history. Around 50% of the European population died by the time the plague reached its climax between 1347 and 1352. It took two centuries for the population to recuperate. European merchants carried several infectious diseases to the completely unprepared American civilizations, hitting them with typhus, measles, and smallpox during the 15th and 16th centuries. The plague returned several times. The first European Influenza pandemic between 1556 and 1560 had a mortality rate of 20%. Even during the 18th century, pandemics were not a stranger. Smallpox killed an estimated 60 million Europeans during the century, especially wiping out infants, with an 80% mortality rate. 30% of the survivors were left blind.

The cities, a result of the agricultural revolution, exposed a weakness of this urban lifestyle. At the same time, as fewer people were poised to work in the agricultural sector, the overall workforce was reduced massively by catastrophic events. The social impact of urbanization and pandemics led to massive social upheaval and religious conflicts. One of the most devastating and destructive of these was the Thirty Years' War. Starting as a struggle between several Protestant and Catholic states, the conflict claimed the lives of eight million people between 1618 and 1648. The factors that led to such a high death count were military activity, famine, violence against civilians, and the plague, as well as other diseases.

The first three industrial revolutions

We are concentrating on Europe at this point because it is where the First Industrial Revolution started. The following was the mixture that formed the foundation for Industrialization:

- Agriculture allowed urbanization and thus provided a workforce and labor market for the secondary sector.
- The farming activities and their intensification in the 15th century generated demand for farming tools and equipment.
- Fiber crops, especially cotton, fueled a new manufacturing activity: textiles.
- Conflicts across Europe made larger scale weapons and ammunition production a must.
- Wars and pandemics reduced the labor force.

In other words, new entrepreneurial activities and higher demand for mechanical products and chemicals met a shrinking workforce. What followed is what we call Industrialization.

CHAPTER SEVEN

Industrialization

Industrialization, the original First Industrial Revolution, created initial shivers in the midst of the 18th century. In the United Kingdom, by 1780 at the latest, the change from agriculture as the dominant driver of the economy to industry being the driving force had started. The UK was ahead of other European nations in global trade as its Empire had colonies in North America, Africa, the Caribbean and the control over the India trade, through the East India Company.

But let us quickly look back at the 400 years leading up to this point. In the year 1337, a series of military conflicts between the Kingdom of England and the French House of Valois started. The issue over which these conflicts were fought was who should rule the Kingdom of France. That question again stemmed from an unfortunate ruling that prevented female succession to the throne of France. With the male lineage of the ruling house ending with the death of Charles IV in 1328, the closest blood relative qualified would have been Edward III of England. His entitlement was questioned and so a conflict started that historians call the Hundred Years' War. In fact, it lasted 116 years, until 1453, ending with a victory for France and its allies.

For England, that was not the end of the conflict. A mere two years later, the War of the Roses began between the House of Lancaster and the House of York, both symbolized by roses – the former red, the latter white. This time the control over the English throne was at stake. The core military activities lasted for around 32 years, ending in 1487, with the extinction of the male lines of both houses.

The economic burden on the population, combined with the drawbacks of feudalism as the form of governance, had become visible throughout the two wars and led to the end of chivalry and pan-European feudalism. The English Renaissance started right after the end of the War of Roses. English language, already traditionally used in literature, got a boost from the invention of the printing press, which also fueled the Protestant Reformation. The Bible, translated by

William Tyndale and published in 1526 in English vernacular, was a further milestone. Culture, expressed in literature, music, and religion became a stronger cohesion element of identity than the allegiance to some king, who randomly ruled due to feudal inheritance rights and intrigues. Nations became a strong driver for identity. Like before in Italy, where the Italian Renaissance had already started in the early years of the 15th century, soon science and a humanitarian view of society was introduced. Sir Francis Bacon published Novum Organum[2] in 1620, advocating a modern, scientific method, rejecting the medieval philosophic way of looking at the world.

While the renaissance created a period of relative peace during the 16th century, war returned around the time when the Baconian Method was adapted.

The modernist forces of Renaissance and science in general, the formation of national identities, the religious tensions due to the Reformation, and the constant battling with pandemics led to a dangerous mixture. The fragmented Holy Roman Empire, holding on to the past, prepared for a final battle to regain control over the future of Europe. With the election of Ferdinand II as the new Emperor, a rather

---

2 Novum Organum translates to 'the new method'

intolerant and counter-reformist ruler took reign. The Protestant states formed the Protestant Union, fearing that the rights of freedom, granted in the Peace of Augsburg, were in danger. Northern and Central European countries under Protestant influence were on high alert. But the rather small Bohemia, mainly Protestant, but under Habsburg Austrian rule and thus part of the Holy Roman Empire, revolted in 1618. This revolt, called the Defenestration of Prague, was the turning point that led to the formation of the Catholic League. It followed an attempt to crush the Protestant rebellion, prompting military action. Soon more and more powers were being pulled into the conflict on both sides, making it a fully-fledged, pan-European war that lasted until 1648, thus giving it the name The Thirty Years' War. It was relative to the size of the population, and in terms of the ratio of civilian vs. combatant fatalities, one of, if not the most, devastating wars in the history of humankind.

The Black Death

At the end of the Middle Ages, Europe was overpopulated; the land factor overtook the labor factor by far. Feudalism cemented this situation. With cities developing and trade routes to the East and West being established, it was just a matter of time before the impoverished strata of society would fall prey to imported diseases. There had been a big plague before, called the Plague of Justinian. It occurred in 541 and 542 and recurred for 200 years, killing an estimated 25 to 50 million people, perhaps a fifth of the world population of the time. Its epicenter was Constantinople, in the Eastern Roman Empire, and from there spread to the port cities around the Mediterranean Sea.

In 1347 the Black Death returned, and again the starting point was Constantinople. This time it had a strong ally; the Hundred Years' War, which started ten years before. The war had weakened the peasantry and also served as a transport vehicle for the pathogen. The marauding troops carried the disease around the continent, like a banner of death. The trade routes around the Mediterranean now had a counterpart in the North with the Hanseatic League, running spacious vessels throughout the Northern and Baltic Seas, further spreading the pandemic. At the highpoint during the first five years, the mortality rate stayed so high that urban populations were often decimated by more than 50%. The European population at the time is estimated to be around 80 million. Less than half of them survived the Plague.

The Black Death

For over 300 years the Plague stayed active, with occurrences somewhere in Europe every single year up to 1671. This continuous presence led to outbreaks, every time humans delivered a good reason for it. The Thirty Years' War started in 1618, and like clockwork, ten years later, the Italian Plague and the French Plague devastated the population between 1628 and 1631. The outbreak led to one million deaths in Italy, with Verona and Milano being hit worst and another million in France.

After that, outbreaks of the Plague became more contained, and Europe step by step was free of the disease. However, it was soon replaced in the 18th century with smallpox, which claimed an average of 400'000 lives per year for the coming 100 years, making it the most significant cause of death during that time.

With the population being continually reduced on such a scale, labor became a scarce economic factor. Both in agriculture and industry, the lack of workers became the dominant bottleneck. At the same time, new industries sprang up that demanded even more workers.

Productivity needed

To gauge the impact of the loss of workforce, just imagine a modern city, say London, and imagine that one in two workers and professionals would vanish. Imagine what that would do to every aspect of the community. The transport system would collapse, the administration could come to a halt, supply chains would get interrupted. The lack of labor force hit the agricultural sector harshly. In the hundred years, between 1350 and 1450, in Germany alone, 40'000 settlements vanished. With the backbone of the workforce eroded, the settlements could not be maintained. It was urgently necessary to lift productivity in the agricultural sector. GDP per capita had been rather stable during the previous centuries. Due to the population growth in the late part of the Middle Ages, the economy grew overall. But now, as the wars had nearly bankrupted most governments in Europe and greatly reduced the number of economically active people, the GDP dropped, both in absolute and per capita terms.

The agricultural sector was understaffed and additionally the weather could quickly make food security a major issue. During the 18th century, there were 15 major famines in

Europe. The two most devastating hit Eastern Prussia in the years 1708 to 1711, killing 250'000 people, or more than 40% of the population, and the 'Grande Famine de France' in the years 1709 and 1710, which killed an estimated 600'000. But also in the late part of the century, famines in Germany, Sweden, Czech lands, and Italy were devastating, leaving hundreds of thousands dead.

The topic so much dominated the headlines that major legislation, engineering, and chemistry efforts were launched to lift land productivity. In Britain, the tide started to turn around 1700, when more and more communally tilled land was privatized. These non-feudal landowners were highly motivated and started to apply modern techniques. Major reforms, like The General Enclosure Act of 1801 ensured that wastelands were turned green and the enterprising new owners drove up yield rates significantly.

This agile approach led to the introduction of the Norfolk four-course crop rotation, as well as the adoption of modernized plows. Dutch contractors that helped with land reclamation from swamps in the Fens of England, brought with them iron-tipped 'Chinese Plows' at the beginning of the century. In 1730, that model, the 'Dutch Plow', was further improved with a cast-iron structure and a cast-iron cover of the entire mouldboard, by Joseph Foljambe. The factory for these plows was set up near Rotherham in England, giving this model its name: the Rotherham Plow. The influence from the relatively densely populated areas of Flanders and Holland was pivotal in several ways. Land reclamation and drainage increased the amount of arable land and allowed former landless peasants to become independent. The idea of water meadows accelerated animal feed production in the early season, driving up milk and fattening rates of cattle, by applying sophisticated irrigation. The introduction of more maneuverable plows, like the Dutch Plow, that could be dragged by only one ox if needed, allowed tilling smaller, irregular patches, and especially lowered the farmer's cost of feeding the draft animals.

Another area of legislation that helped drive productivity up, was the step by step creation of a common market. At the beginning of the 18th century, continental Europe was characterized by thousands of small markets, typically serving a ten-mile radius. Tariffs and tolls, as well as the derelict transport infrastructure, made it more or less impossible to exchange goods between regions. Market presence in larger cities, road or barge transport between those cities, and the elimination of tariffs within Britain created the largest national market in Europe at the time. Already as early as 1700 a national market for wheat existed in the UK. The exchange of regional and seasonal produce between larger city markets let the merchant business flourish. Middlemen were still regulated closely, which was especially necessary for areas such as weights and measures, as well as curbing speculation. However, over time, the restrictive set of regulations was replaced with encouraging rules, pushing for innovation. Britain stayed at the forefront of the Second Agricultural Revolution but also became the cradle of numerous modern commercial techniques, such as auctioning, credit and forward sales, as well as commodity exchanges.

Manure had been used as a natural fertilizer for thousands of years, but its supply was limited. The colonial and global trade activities of Britain provided access to natural fertilizer sources abroad, such as sea bird guano from the Atacama Desert in Chile. In an attempt to create domestic fertilizer, bones from the meat industry were ground up. However, eventually a source of prehistoric fertilizer was uncovered. Botany professor John Stevens Henslow discovered coprolites in Suffolk. These fossilized feces contain phosphate, just as guano does, but it needed to be chemically extracted using sulphuric acid. From the discovery in 1842 to patenting the extraction process to building an industrial-scale activity to refine the so-called 'superphosphate' only some years were needed. Incidentally, within 40 years the industry started declining again. This pattern is an example of the new normal in technology application. While the hand ax invented during the stone age was used for a million years, the window of opportunity for modern inventions became shorter.

Manufacturing

Now that yield rates started to rise and the Second Agricultural Revolution was underway, industrial activities sprang up. These were initially quite a bit about supporting the growing agricultural sector, but also to supply the civil and navy fleets, as well as the rapidly growing transport infrastructure sector on land. By 1760, the shift of labor force from the primary sector to the industry sector was already in full swing. An important material of the time was iron. For hundreds of years charcoal and later hard coal had been used to provide both temperature and carbon for the steelmaking process. The idea to beneficiate the fuel goes back to the fourth century in China. But in Europe, the idea was not known. At the end of the 16th century, many attempts were made to reduce the smell from coal, turf, and peat for household heating and malt roasting in breweries. The higher energy density and more consistent temperature led to the adaptation of the iron smelting process, using such 'cooked coal', or coke for short. In 1709 the first cast iron furnace fired with coke was established near Coalbrookdale. Compared to charcoal, made from wood, which became more and more difficult to obtain, coke was cheaper. Over the decades, the efficiency of the coking process itself improved, driving yield rates from 1/3 to 2/3 of the feedstock, further lowering the fuel cost. This made iron products significantly more competitive.

There had been some practical, but often minimally successful uses of steam since Roman times. This changed in 1712 with the piston steam engine. This external combustion engine used fire to generate steam in a boiler, building up pressure that then gets applied to the end of a cylinder in which a piston is moved. The steam was applied in a cadence that was timed to move a rod back and forth, which then turned an eccentric wheel. The first working model was presented by Thomas Newcomen. In 1720, Jacob Leupold drafted plans for a two-cylinder engine. For quite some time these machines were used in agriculture for irrigation and in mining for water pumping. But the efficiency and effectiveness were not very compelling. This changed with the Watt steam engine, presented by James Watt in 1776. His key idea was the use of a separate condenser, reducing waste energy. The condensation of steam injected into the cylinder was in older designs achieved by spraying the cylinder with cold water. That made the steam condense and thus shrink in volume, creating a partial vacuum. The force of the atmospheric pressure moved the piston, ejecting the condensate. Unfortunately, now the cylinder had to be reheated. That made the stroke frequency painfully slow and wasted a lot of fuel. The separate condenser kept the cylinder hot and ready for the next stroke. This gain in reciprocation frequency was very useful for rotary applications, not just pumping. Watt's improvement meant a gain in energy efficiency, but also a vastly wider field of applications. The steam engine began to displace water wheels and democratized the locations where rotary equipment, for example hammer mills, could be built. Before this industry was limited to locations close to flowing water. Now the engine could be placed anywhere. After further improvements and making the engines lighter, they even became mobile. The Locomobile or traction engine was in principle the first tractor. It helped to replace draft animals for farming needs. The vehicles are sometimes called road locomotives. And indeed, putting a Locomobile onto rails was the groundbreaking idea that made transport of cargo way faster and cost-efficient than ever before. In the year 1802, Richard Trevithick introduced the first working steam locomotive. It was built in the Coalbrookdale ironworks, the very same factory where, for the first time, coke had been used for smelting. The steam locomotive allowed effective, highly scheduled compliant transport of raw materials, semi-finished, and consumer goods between major market locations and areas in the country. The railway quickly became the network that enabled the industrial revolution. It transported the iron ore and thermal coal needed for the steel industry and enabled industrial value chains, sourcing from the entire country and via the ports from overseas. The steam engine itself became the driving force for locomotion, as well as for the mines, blast furnaces, and factories, and eventually the shipping industry.

Now, with sufficient food, higher labor productivity in the agricultural sector, the iron making in full swing, and the steam engine powering transport and factory motion, the groundwork was laid for an ever-growing field of applications for modern manufacturing. It is interesting to note that several chemical and material science discoveries were key to lay the foundation, and so was major progress in

Energization. While the Industrial Revolution is often seen as the hallmark of Mechanization, it was Energization that laid the base for it. It is also remarkable that Industrialization did not 'kill farming'. On the contrary, the need to improve farming due to famine, and thus the necessity for the Second Agricultural Revolution, prepared the path for the productivity gains which allowed the Industrial Revolution.

New industries

Cotton was a fiber crop imported from the colonies, mainly in the Americas back to Europe. While cotton cloth had been a mainstay in China and India for quite some time, Europe had no cotton industry. With the colonial trade this started, and Britain led the way in Europe. In 1750 around 1'200 tons of cotton were imported, spun, and woven, mainly in workers' homes. Merchant weaving shops were practically unknown. The Lancashire region was home to the local weaving industry, which was based around linen and wool. The cottage industry absorbed the new raw material eagerly. 30 years later over 10'000 tons were processed. In 1800, 25'000 tons, and in 1850 over 280'000 tons. By that time, some seven million spindles were in operation. Labor was a key issue. Keeping seven million spindles turning in a country with a population of around 27 million became costly. Indeed the relative productivity[3] compared to India was about half, which made British cotton cloth not exactly cheap.

The cottage industry used the off-season time in the agricultural sector with a typical division of work between merchants providing fiber and taking off the cloth, the women of the household spinning, and the men weaving. It took around four to eight people to spin yarn, to supply what one loom needed. In 1733 John Kay patented the flying shuttle, which together with several other improvements doubled the output of one weaver. Now it took 10 to 15 spinners to work towards one weaver. There were simply not enough women to run the spindles. Innovations were urgently needed. Like in the case of inventing traps to hunt in several places, one worker needed to be empowered to operate several spindles. James Hargreaves, Thomas Highs, and Richard Arkwright made a set of inventions that led to the multi-spindle spinning frame. Here the carding was still manual work, though. In the late 1770s, Samuel Crompton invented the spinning mule, which allowed further

---

3 Relative productivity compares actual productivity, divided by labor cost

productivity gains in the roving and carding process, by combining several processes into one machine. A typical spinning mule would have 1'320 spindles. A mill would be dimensioned to have 60 mules. Each set of two mules could be operated by a minder – an adult – with two boys called the piecers. So the core operation needed 30 minders and 60 piecers. The workweek was 56 hours, exactly the time the machines needed for a fixed set of runs. That added up to over 4.4 million spindle-hours per week. One can imagine how many people in the cottage industry mode would have been needed to perform that amount of work.

Making all these machines and the components, like iron structures, wheels, needles, wires, and the transmission belts was in itself a growing industry. With more and more made of metal, machining was needed to achieve the precision needed within a reasonable amount of time. Machine tools were the solution. Those machines could manage the toolpath in a highly repeatable fashion, compared to freehand tooling. Many of the inventions in this area went back to the needs of innovators in the Realm of Informatization: the clockmakers. Already during the Middle Ages, clockmakers were developing more and more complicated mechanisms. They needed precision. Speed was not yet the motivator. The textile industry in the early part of the Industrial Revolution demanded metal structures for precision but also needed them in numbers that demanded industrial-scale production of components.

In all sectors of manufacturing, the sheer number of motion applications for heavy industry, machining, and assembly was growing at a rate that made the classic steam engine more of a bottleneck than an enabler. The power transmission to the machinery was not easy to control, the steam engines were quite bulky, and especially their efficiency was only between 6 and 10% of the fuel consumed. Solutions were needed to lower the cost of the engine, improve the ease of manufacturing, shrink the footprint, and drive up the energy efficiency. One of those innovations would soon become the beating heart of another innovation. One that would become one of the largest drivers of Industrialization and manufacturing progress: the automobile. And its heart was the internal combustion engine.

Attempts to create steam-powered road vehicles had failed and thus a host of inventors tried to make use of internal combustion, which was supposed to make the size of the engine smaller. Additionally, it did not need a water supply, was less prone to leakages, which were a common problem in steam systems, and intuitively made better use of the fuel. A variety of substances were used for fuels, some exotic, like Lycopodium powder, the spores of a plant related to ferns. It is still being used for fireworks and theatrical effects today. But we should all be glad that it did not become the base of modern individual transport, especially given its limited global harvest. Hydrogen and oxygen mixtures were also tried out and used in what is believed to be the first fully functioning internal combustion engine. The inventor Isaac de Rivaz, a Franco-Swiss, built that in 1804 as a stationary machine. He applied the concept two years later to the first vehicle, propelled by internal combustion. The key limitation was that the hydrogen was supplied from an inflated rubber balloon, which limited the reach considerably. After that it became quite silent around the ICE[4]. De Rivaz's patent eventually became obsolete and it took until 1879 for a meaningful bit of progress to be granted a patent in the ICE propulsion field. This happened when Karl Benz designed his first engine in 1878, and received a patent a year later. Seven years after that the engine powered his Benz Motorwagen over the cobblestone roads of Ladenburg. This idyllic town, nestled at the Neckar River's shore, between Heidelberg and Mannheim, became the place where the first modern car ever

---

4 ICE stands for internal combustion engine

accelerated to a modest top speed. It was his wife Bertha though, who made the first road trip with this car model in 1888, from Mannheim to Pforzheim, covering 66 miles or 106 kilometers one way. We can call this the first road trip with a petrol car ever. And the energy efficiency was above twenty percent, far better than even the most sophisticated steam engine. This was a powerful statement, especially compared to most of the rather short demonstration trips made in competing vehicles. Towards the end of the century, his technology lead made Benz the largest automotive producer in the world, with 572 units produced in one year. The petrol engine would become the cornerstone of the automobile industry, especially for passenger vehicles. Another German, Rudolf Diesel, had been working on a model of an ICE that used a slightly heavier fuel. The Diesel engine, patented in 1892, did not use spark ignition but instead compressed the fuel/air mix enough to trigger self-ignition. This makes for very robust engines. The energy efficiency is still the best of all internal and external combustion principles and can reach 55% in large, two-stroke engines, as applied on ships. The relatively low demands on fuel properties, the simple design, and the high efficiency, made Diesel engines the dominant propulsion system for ships, locomotives, construction equipment, and large trucks.

But there was a completely different idea circulating. And indeed, already in 1881, Frenchman Gustave Trouvé demonstrated a three-wheeled car using electricity. This was during the International Exposition of Electricity in Paris, a brand new event, spun off from the Universal Exposition that had shown some electrical technologies three years earlier. In 1884, Thomas Parker introduced the first production vehicle with electric propulsion in London. Similarly, German Andreas Flocken showed an electric vehicle in 1888. These vehicles used battery technology, which at the time was rather new. They were silent and did not pollute their environment with smoke. Electric motors were even smaller than ICE's and provided a lot of freedom for car designers. But in the end it was easier to build a network of fuel stations for petrol than to come up with the infrastructure to charge batteries across an entire country. So, the inferior technology won the race and became the mainstay for quite some time. Not forever though.

Repercussions

Industrialization was the urgently needed answer to the productivity improvement needs that followed the centuries of wars and epidemics that decimated the labor force and crippled economies. While the precursor, the Second Agricultural Revolution, had little negative side effects, the introduction of large-scale mechanization of work in the secondary sector had numerous impacts. We already discussed the introduction of long weekly work schedules of 60 hours, which deprived the working class of most chances to engage in social, or educational activities. But this was not the only side effect. The huge investments in machinery, especially considering the uncertainty about which production methods would win in the end, made the new class of entrepreneurs quite nervous. They pushed for the lowest cost to speed up payback and the strongest lever for that was paying low wages. The inability to improve yield rates and energy efficiency led to the monoscopic focus on labor cost, thus creating a new class of poor people. This time the cities were affected instead of the rural areas. Only 200 years before subsistence farmers were poor, mainly because they had less to do when harvests were destroyed. They anyway only worked an annual average of around 20 hours a week. But this time around instead of the farmers, it was the workers who became impoverished, with 60 hours of back-breaking work a week. This is the paradox of industrialization; a resource - labor - had to be substituted due to scarcity and then was still priced too low.

The most profound consequence of the new era and the breakneck growth of the industry lay in the very inability to optimize. Industrial activities were enormously wasteful and polluting. Especially during the steam age. The necessary access to infrastructures, such as roads, railroads, canals, and ports, combined with more complex supply chains, commanded the co-location of industrial activities, while workers could not yet be shipped in from afar. Thus living quarters and highly polluting industrial activities had to coexist. This additionally burdened the health situation for the entire population of the rapidly growing cities. In fact, for the first time in almost two centuries, life expectancy went down. There are many ways to define a proxy for the overall health of a population. The average age of death is one, but it lacks comparability since over the time frame of the analysis, military conflict or other disasters distort the demographics. Many researchers thus refer to body height as an indicator of the general public health. The English military painstakingly archived results obtained during recruitment inspections, among which was also data on the height of the soldiers in their early twenties. J. Komlos shows that in 1730 the average height of recruits was about 172 cm. By 1850, at the climax of early Industrialization, it had dropped to 168 cm. While the root causes might be numerous, we can assume that the long work hours, precarious living conditions, and pollution were contributing factors. Similarly, Szreter and Mooney show that life expectancy at birth dropped during that time frame to less than 30 years in Manchester, and even to 25 in Liverpool. Rural areas enjoyed around 20 years of higher life expectancy. We can only guess that a lot of the productivity gains of technology developments were eaten up by lower individual productivity of workers, due to both health impediments and the macro impact of the adverse demographic repercussions. Not only were feedstock and energy wasted, but also human life and workforce.

A characterization of the early industrialization was that resources were wasted and depleted in an even more shortsighted manner than in the following century. Take the example of the coprolite mining mentioned earlier as a source for super-phosphates. The entire mining and chemical extraction process were hard on the environment and the reserves were anyhow rather restricted. After only 40 years the industry vanished. Similarly, in other parts of the world, iron industries were built up based on deforestation for charcoal production. With the forest vanishing around the production plant, the transportation distances and cost went increasingly up, making the investment suboptimal. Or look at the various gold rushes that occurred all around the world. The news of a gold discovery somewhere in the middle of nowhere attracted hosts of soldiers of fortune, gamblers, and whole ecosystems of free riders and service providers, all hoping to find their personal treasure. Whole cities shot up out of the ground, growing rapidly, built recklessly, without a plan and with mediocre infrastructure. Often crime levels shot up and governments lost control. In 1896 gold was found at the Klondike River in Canada's Yukon region. When the message hit large urban areas in the USA, a migration of more than 100'000 prospectors began the perilous trek to the goldfields. On the route, several boomtowns gained importance, such as Dawson City. Its population grew by a factor of 60 within two years. Just another year later the boom was over and many prospectors moved on. Population levels dropped. Enormous amounts of equipment was stranded, the ravaged land left behind in a mess. Most of the indigenous Hän people had been killed or forcibly displaced. Mining peaked in 1903 and then declined. Within less than a decade an unsustainable endeavor was kicked off, peaked, and died.

What drove this way of thinking? What had changed and prompted people to take rushed decisions and bet the farm? Before, for millennia, things were rather foreseeable. Yes, the weather could create issues, even famines. Also, epidemics did strike. But the economic structure and the general direction of business and technology was rather clear. Most of the technological innovations created a benefit wherever they were applied but did not typically generate competitive pressure. The lack of global trade, or even regional trade hid the fact that elsewhere productivity was growing, or products were being improved. With trade activities spanning ever-growing areas, the competition became fiercer. Inferior products or costly production methods could suddenly lead to the extinction of a business that had existed for generations.

The county of Berg, later the Duchy of Berg, in today's lower Rhine area of Germany had iron ore, coal, and a plethora of small rivers and creeks for hydropower. That set the scene for the iron industry and especially the processing industries. Solingen, the famous "City of Blades" is located in the county, and perhaps the best-known manufacturing town in the surrounding area. Based on the tradition of swordsmiths, the capabilities developed to more and more sophisticated precision engineering. Around 1700 the clockmaking industry started. The oldest still-functioning clock from that era was produced by Wilhelm Herder in Solingen in 1715. The production made use of the presence of hydropower and materials from the nearby iron industry. Solingen, Wuppertal, Barmen and other cities in the vicinity had a rich toolmaking tradition, and the craftsmen had accumulated centuries of experience. So all ingredients needed for this new industry venture were at hand. Quickly the number of workshops and brands grew. The ingenious master clockmakers focused their innovation on new features and more challenging complications[5]. Their products were sought after and sold around Europe, adorning palaces, castles, and mansions. Half a century later, another German region, the Black Forest, started to look at the clockmaking industry. Since the use of metal in clockmaking was a privilege for cities under the guild rules of the time, the clockmakers in this rural area resorted to wood as their material. Wood was ubiquitous in the Black Forest, cheap and easy to process. Since anybody was allowed to make wooden clocks, the business became a typical home activity. The

---

5 In horology, a complication means a meaningful feature of a clock or watch. Their complexity is also seen as proof of the abilities of the respective clockmaker.

work-intensive wood processing was done in a large number of small workshops. The formula of success, compared to other areas that also used wood and small wood processing workshops, lay in the presence of several other compatible industries. Instead of manufacturing the entire clock in a workshop, the workshops concentrated on the often playful design and the assembly, while buying in most of the components from other industries, such as bells, chains, gears, and panels. This early Taylorism, or division of work, led to significant productivity gains. The innovation focus was put on process improvements, standardization, and mass fabrication of components. Within just 80 years from its start, the clockmaking industry in the Duchy of Berg was wiped out. The rules of the game had changed. In the Berg area, it took a clockmaker around three weeks to finish a piece. In the Black Forest, a clockmaker needed a full week by 1750. By 1780 he could produce one clock per day. Around 1800 the area produced around 150'000 clocks per year and by 1840 this number had grown to 600'000, which was the majority of the world market at the time. Due to the growth in output, the number of employees had grown tenfold, although the productivity gains were amazing. This typical pattern of vast productivity gains - reducing labor input per unit while still achieving massive growth in output due to cost and thus price reductions – will become a red thread throughout the four Industrial Revolutions. After such a technological innovation wave, a fraction of the original labor is needed to produce a unit. But since the cost drops around the same factor, the market explodes, demanding a multitude of products and driving overall employment in the sector up. At least if you are in the right place. In the Duchy of Berg's clockmaking industry, the craftsman had focused on product features rather than process improvement. Now they needed to find something else to do. No worries, they did.

The fact that the window of opportunity for industrial activities had become short enough for a single generation to see a business take off, peak, and begin to decline, changed the mindset of entrepreneurs forever. Before this, businesses often operated for centuries, passing on from father to son. Clusters, in which a certain craft was predominant, slowly but surely further developed their skills and added additional products. Globalized trade, unsettling such traditions with competing products and a shrinking window of opportunity, created a higher sense of urgency and a feeling of uncertainty. Instead of contemplating how to start up a dynasty in a craft, entrepreneurs considered how to become rich quickly. This might explain the ruthlessness, the gambling mindset, and the high-risk appetite of founders during this time. The treasure hunters of the Klondike, the first chemicals barons in the UK, or the processing industry boom during the Gründerzeit in Germany and Austria are on a different scale but display the same hard-driving mindset. Tough competition, betting on the right technology, the fast speed and quick returns, the high investment needs, and mind-boggling growth, attracted investors who threw money at the founders. The Gründerzeit in Central Europe started more or less with the 1848 revolution, which kicked off a host of liberalization laws. Businesses were set up, benefiting from political reforms. Citizens became the driving force for cultural developments during this time of classical liberalism. Additionally, after the Franco-Prussian War of 1870/71, large war reparation payments flooded into the German-speaking part of Europe. The situation heated up and the funds were thrown at any and every industrial venture, bubbling up to the Gründer-crash. In 1873, first the Vienna stock market collapsed, toppling over other European stock exchanges and igniting the Panic of 1873 in America. Like in Europe, investors had made huge bets, mainly in the railroad industry. After the bloody Civil War ended in 1865, the country strove to interconnect its vast area, and the railroad offered just the means to do that. The investments were huge, often competing, and highly speculative. With the ripples from Europe and several homemade issues destabilizing the situation, the finance system crashed. The symbol of this crash in the US was the default of Jay Cooke & Company. Cooke had set out to finance a competing transcontinental railroad, the Northern Pacific Railway. Monetary policies under the administration of President Ulysses S. Grant aimed to cool down the overheated economy by contracting the money supply, thus driving interest rates up. Cooke started to tumble and fell on September 18, 1873. A chain reaction followed; banks failed and the New York Stock Exchange closed for 10 days on September 20. Within a year, over 100 railroad companies folded their cards. The whole industry collapsed, with new rail tracks laid falling by almost 80%. The whole ecosystem of suppliers around it shook and within two years over 18'000 other businesses failed in the wake of the railroad crash. What followed was the so-called Long Depression, a worldwide recession lasting for over a decade.

CHAPTER EIGHT

Electrification

I n spite of the side effects and ugly excesses of the First Industrial Revolution, over time it improved the economic situation of the working class, particularly through job creation and rising salaries. Paying workers well also became affordable for employers due to the vast productivity gains. Societies and legislators understood that occupational health and safety was not only good for the individual worker, but also the overall economic system. Big strides were made to reduce working hours, improve work safety, and concentrate industrial activities, away from residential compounds. As a result of the industrial revolution of the 19th century, governments had the means to build and grow national level infrastructure. The methodologies of serial manufacturing and division of work, as well as standardization, with its immense savings potential, allowed it to make many products affordable for the masses. For the first time consumption became a mass phenomenon. People who before had nothing more than their daily bread and clothes on their body started to possess household durables, decorative items, and even personal transportation means. For the overwhelming part that meant, of course, owning a bicycle. The internal combustion engine had taken over for commercial propulsion needs, signaling the end of the steam engine, which only persevered for some more decades in the railroad industry.

The advantages of the electric motor were very clear though, and for stationary applications, the battery charging was no major issue or could be replaced by a direct connection to the power grid. The factories of the First Industrial Revolution needed hundreds or thousands of actuators. Combustion engines would have created massive pollution in the factory buildings. The fuel supply would have become a nightmare for logistics and safety, not to mention the infernal noise. Using combustion engines also meant that mechanical transmission via line shafts and belts or chains was needed, which was inefficient, expensive, unsafe, and which made the modification of production lines quite cumbersome. The Paris International Exposition of Electricity was amongst the first dedicated to this new, up-and-coming technology that would usher in the Second Industrial Revolution: Electrification.

But before the broad-based creation of a power grid for transmission and distribution of electric power, electricity was rather used in a completely different context than Energization. The reason for that was twofold. It was still difficult to generate large amounts of electric power, and it was still not feasible to create networks touching every little town and even bridging the last mile to the individual commercial or residential consumption points. So what was it that could be done already? Using very little power and only building a point-to-point network to major town centers. In other words, using electricity for an application within the Realm of Informatization. We are talking about the telegraph. In the 1840s the first so-called needle telegraphs were installed. They were based on an invention by William Cooke and Charles Wheatstone. The operator in the sending office had to punch buttons that transmitted a pulsed signal over the wire to a receiving office, where an electromagnetic actuator, a so-called needle pointer, marked the message upon a paper strip. In other words, this first application did not actually help with Energization or Mechanization at all but was a way to transmit information and to store that information on a paper strip in a faraway place. No wonder this technology enjoyed massive adoption and investment. Soon "the wires" were an integral part of society and daily life. Telegraphs were used by business people, journalists, and of course the government and the military. And very typical for any innovation in the Realm of Informatization, inventors quickly addressed the speed of information transmission, error prevention, and simplicity of the hardware. While the first systems used five wires to generate combinations of signals that were interpreted as letters, Samuel Morse from Charlestown, Massachusetts, already proposed a coding system in 1838. It allowed using only one wire and two base signals, short and long. Combinations of that represented the letters. The system saved a lot of money and it was far easier to create redundancy. And it allowed to not only encode the message on a paper strip. Instead, a telegraph sounder made two distinct sounds for short and long, and operators were able to decode the message on the fly, writing it down in plain text. Imagine, an existing five wires connection, could now be used for five transmissions in parallel. The cost factor of reducing the number of wires needed was especially important for an application that had a rather globalizing effect: submarine cables. Some years after the first deployments of telegraphic lines, tests were done in the New York Harbor, submersing cables in water to transmit signals. The insulation material was a latex impregnated hemp tissue, tightly wrapped around the copper wire. The idea was based on experiments conducted during the early 19th century by Moritz von Jacobi, a German-Russian engineer. And indeed, it worked. The leakage of current was low enough to have the signal preserved, even across significant distances. Soon other materials were tested. Amongst them Gutta-percha made from the sap of the Palaquium plant, found mainly in India. While latex rubber is a biological duroplastic material, meaning once applied it keeps its shape, Gutta-percha is in fact a biological thermoplast. Which means, application of heat makes it soft again, which enables it to mold itself even closer around a conductor. The first test of such an insulation material on a submarine cable happened in 1845 between Cologne and Deutz, crossing the Rhine river. That was the dry run for the Dover Calais connection crossing the British Channel. In 1859 the concession was granted, though the first attempt using a simple Gutta-percha covered wire failed. Two years later the first true cable was laid. It contained the insulated signal wire, and was additionally surrounded by a core protection that added to the mechanical and electrical strength. It was a success and interconnections between Belgium, the Netherlands, Germany, Denmark, and Ireland followed soon. In 1866 the SS Great Eastern, then the largest steam powered vessel on Earth, completed laying the first reliable transatlantic cable. Later she also laid the first cable connecting via Aden in Yemen to India. The colonial empire of Britain, which provided both supplies of materials and the need for global communication, together with its investment strength and technological acumen, brought Britain into a dominant position in this new industry. Until 1911, the British cables monopolized the transatlantic connection. Already at that time first fears surfaced of what would happen in case of a conflict. Wires or cables running through enemy territory could easily be cut or tapped. The British Empire worked on the "All Red Line", a network using British territories only, connecting all members of the Empire and all major trade partners of Britain. And indeed, cyber warfare was practiced when World War I broke out. The moment that Britain declared war on Germany, the cable-laying ship Alert was dispatched to cut the five cables linking Germany with Spain, France, and via the Azores with North America. Dominance in this new field was economically as well as militarily important. In the 1890s British companies owned twenty-four of the world's thirty cable-laying vessels, and two-thirds of all cables.

On to the next major application of electricity. And again, it is not about motion or Energization. In the early 19th century, Italian chemist Luigi Valentino Brugnatelli made use of his friend's battery, a voltaic pile. Alessandro Volta had created the first useful battery by stacking zinc and copper plates with a salt water electrolyte around them. The battery provided a continuous electric current. This allowed numerous experiments. Though Brugnatelli received heavy backlash from the scientific establishment and his ideas were forgotten for around 30 years, eventually it was again Moritz von Jacobi who unearthed the previous work on electrochemistry. In 1838 he showcased his new invention: galvanoplasty or electrotyping. This method allows the creation of an exact facsimile of any object, regardless of whether regular or irregular. A mold is formed from the model. It can be made of wax, latex, or paraffin. The mold's surface is then sprayed with a very fine layer of graphite paint, creating a conductive surface. When the mold is suspended into an electrolyte bath, with the minus pole of a DC source connected to it, the current flowing through an anode material, such as copper, oxidizes that. That means copper ions are broken out of the anode and the current transports the ions towards the mold, where they deposit. Over time the copper layer gets thicker. Once it reaches the desired strength, the process is halted and the mold material gets removed. The copper form is a replica of the original model, with a perfect, smooth surface. Jacobi used the technique first for artwork. Quite some "bronze" sculptures are in reality copper galvanoplastic. For large sculptures, making the mold from a cheap and easy to manipulate material such as wax was a massive accelerator, compared to the expensive molds for bronze casting. Also, the control over material strength, surface quality, and detail was superior and it saved significant amounts of material. As we know, art is part of the Realm of Informatization and so is the major application of galvanoplasty, called electrotyping. The name indicates that the technique has to do with printing. When the model is made of movable lead types, the result of the galvanoplasty process is a perfect print plate. Once that is made, the lead types can immediately be reused for the next plate, and so on. Since the copper layer is thin and on top of a pliable material, such as Gutta-percha, the print plate can be bent and affixed onto a roller for offset printing. But also normal sheet printing was, of course, possible and used for art reproductions. Electrotyping was the most important enabler for modern offset printing and thus the proliferation of newspapers and magazines. While the telegraph connected the reporters and correspondents to the publishing houses in near light speed[6], the fast production of electrotyped plates allowed the printing houses to keep that pace and to have the articles printed overnight, so they were in the newspaper the next morning already. Another example of innovation in the Realm of Informatization, using Electrification as the foundation.

As we saw before, electrochemical processes allow plating an object with an anode material. Besides electrotyping, another use of this effect is to plate an object instead of an expendable mold. The aim here is to change the characteristics of that object. A variety of combinations of anode materials and plating baths allow electroplating metal objects, but also non-metal objects with an even and quite perfect layer of the anode material. Metallic elements such as copper, zinc, nickel, silver, and gold, as well as alloys such as brass or solder can be deposited. The useful effects vary, from aesthetic appearance, corrosion resistance, conductivity, tensile strength and surface hardness to contact resistance. Especially corrosion protection and the surface hardening in tool production were essential for the progress of

---

6 Actually: telegraph signals, being electricity in a normal conductor, move with the hundredth part of light speed. US coast to coast in one second.

Industrialization. First patents for what is called electroplating were granted to the Elkington cousins from Birmingham, who founded the electroplating industry in their hometown. Soon batteries were replaced with generators to allow larger scale and longer plating sessions. The Woolrich Electrical Generator, built in the year 1844, was acquired by the Elkington's and was the first example of the transition from batteries to generators in the electrochemical industry. In 1876 the Norddeutsche Affinerie started production in Hamburg, Germany. It was the first modern, large scale electroplating plant in the world.

The next decade saw a true example of Energization finally having a breakthrough: electric lighting. The first trials by Sir Humphry Davy go back to 1802. But his light arc between two carbon electrodes was at the time not practical. It generated huge amounts of heat and sparks, needed constant adjustment, and presented a hazard. In 1850 William Petrie presented a self-regulating version that at least found some pilot applications, such as the National Gallery in London. It was only a novelty, though. Later on, Pavel Yablochkov improved the design further, and cut out the need for a regulator altogether. The lamp was showcased at the Paris Expo in 1878 and installed in some iconic locations in the city. The installations used a Gramme generator, invented by the Belgian inventor Zénobe Gramme. These generators used a ring-shaped armature, where coils could be placed in different locations and wired together as poles. With this, the average amplitude of the current and the overall smoothness of the generated current could be improved the more coil pairs and poles were applied. This combination of a lower maintenance arc lamp and the Gramme generator, convinced Rookes E.B. Crompton from Yorkshire, to take electric lighting seriously. He further improved the designs and his lamps created a brighter and more steady light. He founded Crompton & Co in 1878 and began mass production of electrical goods. Both its own inventions and licensed products were produced and Crompton & Co managed to cover the entire portfolio of known technologies, establishing the company as the first electrical engineering firm in the history of mankind. Crompton understood that to drive sales for his lamps, he had to provide the generation equipment, wires, terminations, and so on. He also looked for ideas to present further products that consumed electricity. The first widely accepted electric oven, the first bread toaster, and many other appliance innovations entered the marketplace at this time.

For widespread street lighting and residential applications, the lamps needed to become more economic, longer living, and easier to install. Incandescent lights were demonstrated over and over with a variety of materials for the filaments and lead-ins. They all suffered from a key problem - the presence of oxygen in the air destroyed the filaments, which simply burned away. Lodygin received a patent in Russia for a lamp with Nitrogen filled glass ampule, which improved the longevity. But it was British physicist Joseph Wilson Swan who came up with the idea to evacuate the bulb to suppress oxidation. In 1878 he received a patent in England for this lamp, which had a special socket, the Swan socket, which compared to others was resilient to vibrations, a problem in vehicles. A key technology component for the mass production of vacuum-based light bulbs was the vacuum pump, needed to quickly evacuate the bulb during the manufacturing process. Swan used the mercurial pump, invented in 1865 by Hermann Sprengel, from Hannover, Germany. Sprengel was a chemist and interested in studying the effects of vacuum on chemicals. As a chemist, he had access to mercury and his work was laboratory type work. In the absence of a better solution, lamp manufacturers settled with the Sprengel pump. But it was not exactly suitable for scaling the production from lab to fab. Adolph Berrenberg, born in Marienheide, a small village in the Duchy of Berg, made several improvements and was closely associated with several lamp manufacturers in his homeland as well as in America, to where he immigrated in the notorious year 1878. The most important advantage of his method was that it replaced the mercury used before as "liquid" piston. Mercurial pumps used the weight and chemical properties of mercury to aid the evacuation process. Bubbles traveling back through the mercury degraded the result, but most importantly, handling these amounts of the highly poisonous mercury was highly hazardous. The Berrenberg patent-based pumps of the Beacon Vacuum Pump and Electrical Company from Boston were able to evacuate 600 lamps at once, within less than an hour, while mercurial pumps only managed six lamps within five hours. This was an enormous productivity gain, and a great step towards making the production less dangerous.

Two years after Swan, Thomas Alva Edison filed a patent for more or less the same development. Later on, they agreed on a cooperation. While Edison is clearly not the inventor of the incandescent light bulb, he did improve the production process. By driving up the precision of the filament making, he was able to create high resistance filaments. This meant that the lamp could be powered with a lower current on a higher voltage level. Raising the voltage in distribution systems was key to reduce losses and the needed diameter of wires and cables. Transforming voltage up meant transporting energy with less current and more voltage, and current is responsible for losses in a power network. In the first networks, these losses were countered by dimensioning the copper wire thick enough to lower its resistance, and thus losses. That made the distribution infrastructure expensive. Once changing to higher voltages, the networks quickly became cheaper than the competing gas pipes for gas lamps. Besides that, Edison's lamps were suitable to share a generation source amongst many lamps, while older models needed a separate Gramme generator for a handful of lamps. Edison also realized that workshop scale was not enough and set up the first dedicated light bulb factory for mass production. Again, like in the case of the clocks, innovation in the production process was decisive in winning the race and made the Edison Company the leading manufacturer of light bulbs for an extended period.

Now the time was right for the synchronized growth of the entire ecosystem of generation capacities, distribution grids, and revenue-generating, broad-based consumption of electricity. Electric light was the first product of this ecosystem - a classic Energization application. Now it was possible to use the kinetic energy of water driving a turbine to create light in a place a hundred miles away. The late years of the 19th century were the start of the Second Industrial Revolution: Electrification. It meant both presenting new applications and also replacing existing technologies, like gas lamps, with electricity. Throughout the centuries, electricity would go on to replace one technology after another. The future of our civilization is electrical.

Generation

Electricity occurs in nature. In the cloud systems of thunderstorms, the opposite movement of sinking graupel[7] and rising ice crystals causes billions of collisions, during which the ice crystals accumulate a positive charge, while the graupel gets charged negatively. As a result, a thundercloud represents a giant electrostatic generator. Electrostatic systems carry very high voltages but do not deliver a lasting electric current. In the case of a typical negative discharge during a thunderstorm, a lightning bolt still generates an impressive current of around 30'000 amperes, in some cases up to 120'000 amperes. The rarer positive discharges can reach even 400'000 amperes. The typical electric protection

---

7 Graupel is a form of soft hail that forms pellets with a snowflake at their centers.

systems in peoples' homes cap currents at ten amperes. No wonder lightning strikes can be lethal to buildings and humans alike. The whole discharge lasts for around 200 microseconds[8]. During this short glimpse, the average lightning bolt delivers 500 megajoules of energy. That is the same energy that is stored in around 30 kg of sugar or a fifth of a barrel of crude oil. With one to two billion lightning strikes per year around the planet, thunderstorms transform on average the energy value of around 280 million barrels of oil every year. It sounds like a great deal, but it is less than 4 days of global oil production. Compare that to solar irradiation. The sun needs only 6 seconds to radiate the same amount of energy onto the earth's surface. Lightning is impressive and has always frightened humans. It does start fires, and that allowed our ancestors to capture and control fire during the early times of the Second Realm of Innovation. But otherwise, it does not play a big role in the progress of our civilization.

Where electricity does play a huge role in nature is inside biological life forms. The nervous system of animals uses a mix of chemical and electrical mechanisms to transmit signals. Neurons, the nerve cells, are like the internal wiring

---

8 A microsecond represents one millionth part of a second.

of the body. They can collect sensory input, but can also transport motor commands to the muscles. And, of course, they form the brain with all its control and thinking capability. The electric signals are produced, in the exact moment of sending information, by a bio-electrochemical process. The bodies of most animals do not store electricity. But there are exceptions. Some fish species feature a special kind of cell, so-called electrocytes. Those derived evolutionarily from motor neurons and muscle cells. A stack of such cells uses ATP[9], the body's basic chemical energy, which is normally needed by muscles to conduct work, to instead push sodium and potassium ions through the cell membrane. As a result, these ions form now a positively charged cloud around the stack. The similarity to a voltaic pile - a battery - is stunning. The firing is triggered by a pacemaker nucleus, a bundle of pacemaker neurons, similar to the sinus node that controls the heartbeat. Electric eels and electric rays are strongly electric fish. They use the electric fields they produce for several purposes - in a weak form, for locating prey, and in a strong form to stun the prey. A heavy impulse is also used as a self-defense measure.

---

9 Adenosin Triphosphate: a bio-chemical that living beings use to readily store energy.

Compared to primary energy, like hydrocarbons or solar radiation, nature does not provide us with useful amounts or forms of electricity. This secondary energy needs to be derived from primary sources. This is the reason why the Second Industrial Revolution needed some time to pick up speed. Only once Mechanization provided a strong enough portfolio of its technologies, Energization could use these as building blocks for electricity generation. The main breakthrough was to use Michael Faraday's principles on the electromagnetic motion. First the DC machine was improved, by Wheatstone, Siemens, and Varley during the 1860s, and finally the understanding grew that AC[10] systems would have significant economic advantages. The alternator, or synchronous generator, was introduced during the 1880s with major contributions from James E.H. Gordon and William Stanley Jr., with Westinghouse Electric. Alternators produce AC power, which is easier to transform up to high voltage levels. As we discussed earlier, when transporting energy in power systems, this can be done by voltage and by the current. Electric power is the product of voltage drop multiplied by the flow of current. The resistance of the conductors, the cables and wires, hampers the flow of the

---

10 Alternating Current

current, creating losses. Therefore, the same amount of power can be transmitted with lower resistive losses when the voltage is high, allowing the necessary current to be lower. The technology component used to drive the voltage up is called a transformer. Transformers use induction coils. When a current flows through the primary coil, which has a small number of windings, a magnetic field is induced. The energy is now stored in the magnetic field. When the current is interrupted, the field collapses, inducing a current in the secondary coil, which sits on the same core. The secondary coil is built with a multitude of thinner windings, and the resulting current cannot build up to the same level as it was in the primary coil. The energy of the magnetic field thus induces a higher voltage to deliver that same amount of energy. Powering such an inductive coil with DC power means that an interrupter is needed to switch the DC power off for a short moment, to trigger the collapse of the magnetic field. The result is a short, high voltage impulse. This can be used to create a spark, for example in the spark plugs for combustion engines. This is not an efficient way to create smooth, high voltage electricity for distribution. When instead such a transformer is fed with AC power, the sinus waveform of the alternating current lets the magnetic field grow and shrink, inducing a smooth, high voltage wave on the side of the secondary coil. The absence of the interrupter makes the system a lot more reliable. There is another aspect that made AC a superior solution. When something goes wrong in a high-powered electrical system, say a short circuit or a transmission wire dropping to the ground, the amount of energy the faulty system draws can grow enormously. In such cases, the current needs to be interrupted. You could say the system needs a kind of emergency shut down. This is performed with so-called power circuit breakers. A breaker is normally closed and current flows through. When an operator or an automatic protection system senses a fault, the breaker is activated and creates a gap in the conductor that splits the network, so that the flow of current is stopped. This leads to a temporary surge in voltage, which can jump over that gap, forming a burning arc of plasma. On a small scale, such an arc was deliberately provoked and used in the first electric lamps, before the invention of the light bulb. In the large scale of a power utility system, this arc becomes a self-sustaining menace. Super hot plasma, consisting of ionized gas, creates a highly conductive channel that keeps the current flowing while feeding on it. The plasma destroys the breaker, while the fault itself, not being switched off, destroys other assets connected to the system. In an AC system, the breaker gets some help, though. Since the alternating current oscillates between positive and negative, it passes through a zero point in the sine curve. That is the moment the breaker mechanism uses to further distance the poles, until the arc breaks. In a high-voltage DC system, this is a lot more difficult. For a long time, it was seen as the final riddle of power systems. Until ABB, the pioneer in HVDC[11] systems, introduced the world's first HVDC breaker in 2012, more than a century later than the commercialization of HVAC breakers.

So transformers are a key element for the practicality of a power system and especially the energy efficiency of the transmission of power. In the notorious year 1878, Hungarian company Ganz started producing a variety of electric products in Budapest, installing systems in both Austria and Hungary. It was Ganz that became the first company to produce efficient AC transformers, called ZBD transformers, using the first letters of the names Zipernowsky, Blathy, and Deri, the three engineers at Ganz who invented the so-called closed-core transformer. Compared to open-core transformers, these were more than three times as efficient. The first unit shipped in September 1884. Westinghouse, not having access to the ZBD patents, came up with their own

11 HVDC is an acronym for High Voltage Direct Current.

version, which emphasized ease of manufacturing using prewound cores and first sold in 1886. In 1889, AEG[12] of Germany introduced the first three-phase transformer, developed by their genius engineer Mikhail Dolivo-Dobrovolski. He also invented the three-phase generator and the three-phase motor in 1888. Dolivo-Dobrovolski, born in Russia, who emigrated to Germany because of political reasons, studied at the Technical University of Darmstadt, and later joined AEG. In 1891, during the International Electrotechnical Exhibition in Frankfurt, Germany, for the first time, a long-distance, three-phase system was demonstrated. Since Frankfurt did not have its own power station, power was deliberately taken from a hydropower plant in Lauffen at the Neckar river and transmitted over 175 km to Frankfurt. When visitors entered the fairgrounds, they stepped through an arch, carrying a sign "Power Transmission Lauffen-Frankfurt 175 KM", with the logos of AEG and MFO (Maschinenfabrik Oerlikon, later part of BBC) to the right and left. The system generated 300 horsepower, three-phase electricity on 55 volts. A three-phase transformer took that up to 8'000 volts, feeding the three-phase transmission line. The power arrived with an efficiency

---

12 Allgemeine Elektricitäts-Gesellschaft (general electric company).

of 75% in Frankfurt. It powered thousands of light bulbs, the three-phase motor pump for an artificial waterfall, and dozens of exhibits. With 1.2 million visitors from all over the world, the exhibition was an absolute breakthrough and - first in Germany, then worldwide - the decision for AC as the efficient means for power infrastructure was taken, ending the "War of Currents" between DC and AC promoters.

Now that the basic ground rules were clear, utility companies sprang up to build generation plants all around the world. There was a never-ending evolution of generation methods. Electricity generation is perhaps the most allegorical example of the Realm of Energization. It means converting whatever form of energy we find, using transformation machinery, into a flow of electric current. That electric current can then be used for almost limitless applications in motion, light, and information. There are three fundamental mechanisms known to mankind to accomplish electrical power generation. Electricity can be directly produced from a chemical reaction. Electrochemical reactions are used for example in batteries and fuel cells. This was the earliest known technology for electricity generation. It mimics the processes in living organisms, using electricity for nervous system operations. In the late 18th century, this was the only way to create a sustained electrical current. In the early 19th century, the photovoltaic effect was added as a second way to generate electricity. In 1839 Edmond Becquerel was the first to observe that light was able to create voltage and current when illuminating electrodes of silver chloride coated platinum. The effect was later named after its 19-year-old discoverer. Much later the technology would be refined, driving the efficiency way up and making PV solar power one of the most viable generation technologies. Direct conversion of light into another form of energy is what plants use in photosynthesis. The advantage of that is that the energy is captured in a storable form. While elegant, photovoltaic systems were at the time not yet suitable for scaling up. It is a curious fact that Becquerel was actually working on progressing a technology branch within the Realm of Informatization when making his discovery. Young Edmond was keen to improve photography, and thus was experimenting with substances used for photochemical image capturing.

It is also interesting that neither electrochemical nor photoelectrical phenomena were part of the early breakthrough of power generation. Today, batteries and fuel cells are the core of the future of electromobility and solar cells the core of the renewable energy revolution. But at the beginning, it would be the electromechanical principle that allowed scale, economy, and was able to mobilize acceptance of the existing heavyweights in industry. Electromechanical generation means that a kinetic energy source is used to drive an electromagnetic generator. So what contributed to the success of this third and so far last fundamental generation type? First of all, there are a number of kinetic energy sources that can be used to turn the shaft of a generator. It can be a treadmill that is moved by human force or draft animals, a windmill, a water wheel, or an existing steam engine. Any internal combustion engine, stationary or mobile, would also work. The latter made it possible to have auxiliary electric power on board cars, trains, vessels, and even airplanes. What helped with the scaling up were hydropower plants. They used similar locations as the old mechanical mills, often even shared water infrastructure with them. The proximity to the existing industrial users was beneficial. They used renewable primary energy, which took operational cost down. Wherever sufficient hydro resources were not present, the method of choice was thermal power generation. Like in the case of the steam engine, fuel was used to create heat, boil water, and use the steam to drive a mechanical system. In 1884, Sir Charles Parsons demonstrated the first steam turbine. It had 7.5 kilowatts. That was soon scaled up by George Westinghouse to 50 kilowatts. Parsons would, during his life, see his invention scaled up to 100 megawatts. The advantage of the steam turbine was its efficiency versus the steam piston engine, and the scalability versus internal combustion engines. Also, that the process of steam generation could be based on a whole range of technologies and fuels. That allowed the use of coal, geothermal energy, nuclear processes, or even concentrated solar power to generate the necessary steam. Even the hot exhaust gas of a newer invention, the gas turbine, could be scavenged to drive a connected steam turbine. The gas turbine system was simpler and used natural gas or biogas. That allowed for compact, lower emission plants. Whoever had been busy making engines, water infrastructure, metal structures, or locomotives, liked thermal power generation. Electrochemical and photovoltaic systems did not have friends like that.

While the individual size of plants was growing, driving economy of scale up, the annual output did not grow that massively in the early decades of the 20th century. Take Germany, one of the large economies and pioneers in electrification. Until 1950, the annual output did not even reach 50 terawatt hours. Before 1960 it jumped to 100 TWh and during the next two decades it doubled again every ten years, reaching over 400 TWh in 1980. After that the growth slowed again. 1950 to 1980 saw exponential growth and the true breakthrough. Similar developments can be observed throughout the developed world. The next question was how best to coordinate the delivery of all that power.

Transmission and Distribution

Electricity is an enormously versatile form of energy. Once the generation process is finished, the result – secondary energy – can be used for limitless applications: motion, light, telecommunication, heating, cooling, air conditioning, entertainment systems, material treatment. Electricity can be transported across long distances and distributed finely, touching on every room in every building of a city. But since storing electricity in large amounts is a challenge, the generation, transport, and consumption needs to be synchronized. That is easier when there are many producers and consumers connected in one network. This drives up the reliability of the supply and smooths out the demand curve. The reliability is needed since the users do not have buffers, as they used to have with primary fuels. The demand needs to be smooth, since over- or underconsumption creates issues for the generator and alters the frequency in AC networks, which in turn creates issues for many consumption assets. The frequency needs to stay within a rather small band around the standard, typically 50 or 60 hertz. This is best achieved the larger the synchronized network is.

Initially, transmission networks, spanning long distances, were not primarily meant to increase reliability, but rather to connect different generation assets to maximize economy. In Europe that meant to connect the alpine hydropower assets with the lowland thermal coal generation plants. The idea was to maximize renewable energy, to save fuel. In Europe this started with the North-South connection within Germany, but during the 1940s further countries were interconnected. In 1951 eight European countries met in Paris to form the UCPTE. 1987 four further countries were added. In 1995 the interconnection with the East-European CENTREL system added another four countries. In 2019 24 countries are represented in the UCTE. The "P" was dropped when, after the market liberalization, the producers were separated from the transmission system operators. The UCTE network provides power to 450 million people, supplying over 2'500 TWh per year, which makes it the largest synchronized network in the world. In terms of peak demand, the Eastern Interconnection in North America is the largest network, reaching over 700 GW during summertime. Such huge synchronized networks consist of millions of assets, tens of thousands of kilometers of lines, and are spread out over millions of square kilometers, touching on enormous amounts of productive assets that represent a huge part of the economy within their respective territory. We can say that such networks are the largest human-made machines that are controlled and coordinated as one system. There are other infrastructure assets that span huge regions, such as road networks, but there is no central control of the traffic on such networks. The challenge to centrally control, optimize, and operate a synchronized power network in a reliable and efficient way is one of the largest tasks managed by humankind.

Electricity in developed countries is so ubiquitous and reliable that we do not even think about it. Due to the standardization in terms of voltage level and frequency, it is easy to design products or applications that use electricity. The standardization in the power grid and distribution system on the last mile was the blueprint for other network type technology rollouts in the telecommunications sector, information services, and entertainment systems. This is a big difference between Mechanization and Electrification. In Mechanization, the core of progress lies in individual plants, using specialized equipment, producing a differentiated product. In Electrification the strength lies in the compatibility of standardized products, made by a networked system of assets. Compatibility beats competitiveness, in this case. At a later stage, when it is already a de facto standard, elements of competition can be introduced into a networked system. Whether that bears fruit for consumers depends on how exactly it is done and whether distortions of the playing field are avoided. Investments in generation assets are quite comparable to investing in any other production facility. The more you produce and the tighter the operational discipline, the better the return on investment. If you have a bad day, revenues drop a bit. Your entire plant is within a fence, on premise, so to speak. Most staff is on that single site as well. Assets, people, and processes are within the control sphere of the plant operator. And capacity is very much controlled by the investor as well, who tries to avoid overcapacity. On the other hand, transmission and distribution assets are spread out, often sitting on other owners' land. Utilization depends on the interplay of generation assets, consumers, and the overall load management within the synchronized grid. The key product is the reliability of the system and that grows with the density of nodes. A node in a power network is an intersection of two or more power lines or cables. The more nodes a grid has the more it is intermeshed. That drives up reliability by providing alternative routes for power, in case of a disturbance in a line. Providing such redundancy does not grow the transaction volume or value of the power transmitted, but grows the asset base and thus the cost. Assets outside of the control sphere are more difficult to manage in terms of supervision, risk management, and maintenance. From the very beginning, T&D operators began to cover the power network with telecommunication systems. That also happened for railway networks, where signaling, as well as station-to-station communication, and the remote operation of track switches were needed. The difference lies in the necessary speed. Whether a railway signal is switched a second or even a couple of seconds earlier or later does not matter that much. In T&D networks switching and especially protection activities need to be conducted in hyper-real time. Since electricity travels with some 3'000 km per second and so called transient short circuit currents ramp up extremely quickly, it is important to detect a fault during the first milliseconds and switch it off during the first or second zero crossing of the sine curve. In a 50 Hertz system, a zero crossing happens 100 times per second - you can imagine how fast the algorithms and actuators need to be to interrupt fast enough. With the introduction of renewable energy, with numerous distributed feed-in points and the overall distribution of generation assets, the system-wide short circuit current grows, making ultrafast protection systems even more important.

Electricity and the future

We saw that electricity did not always win right away. In motion applications for industrial purposes, Industrialization rather relied on steam and the automotive sector on petrol. But eventually electricity reconquers many segments of the market. There are three main properties of electricity that come into play: versatility, standardization, and risk manageability.

Let us look at the most promising competitor first: gas. The closest rival for electricity of all energy sources would be gas. Fuel gases, whether natural gas, biogas, or syngas are highly standardized and quality levels can be kept within a narrow band. That means chemical composition, energy content, and physical properties are prescribed and ensured. These properties also do not change; they don't degrade. Gas is suitable for storing energy. Gas can, in fact, be economically stored in two physical states - in gaseous and liquid form. Liquefaction allows the transport and storage of large quantities of gas in tanks, bottles, cartridges, and onboard transport vessels for road, rail, and sea transport. Storage again does not degrade the quality of the fuel and allows, more or less, infinite stockpiling. Also, the transmission and distribution through pipelines is possible, economic, and practical. This allows bringing gas from bulk sources to individual users reliably and continuously. With electricity, storing is a lot more difficult. Batteries have for the longest time only been suitable for small-scale applications, such as mobile devices, handheld torches, and on-board auxiliary power. For large-scale storage, the reversion of the generation process, for example by the way of pumped-storage water reservoirs, is needed, thus the storage form is actually the original primary energy source of the electrical energy. In summary, gas can be transported in many more ways than electricity, packaged in a variety of useful containers, or brought to consumers by a network. Stockpiling, local buffering, and storage are all possible, unlike with electricity. Similar to electricity, there are several ways to derive gas. It can be explored as naturally occurring gas, synthesized in chemical plants, or harvested from renewable biomass sources by fermentation. The perceived risks around handling gases perhaps put gas at a slight disadvantage. Take the United States, a country that uses relatively more natural gas than other countries. Around every second day, an incident with gas transmission and distribution occurs in the US, killing around a dozen people during a typical year. With 3.9 million kilometers of gas pipelines and around 180 million consumers using this fuel, this is - though tragic - a relatively low number. Compare it, for example, to statistically around 400 fatalities per year due to electrocution in the US. Even if the two are not fully comparable, it illustrates that gas is not per se the higher risk energy. So gas is practical, available, can be stored, and the risk profile is roughly the same. What gave electricity the winning edge? Let us look at what can be done with gas. Gas is very suitable for any application with heating involved: central heating in buildings, ovens in industrial and kitchen applications, stoves, even small scale blow torches. It can be used for lighting, which was the original first application. Even cooling is possible. Gas-powered refrigerators are still being used on boats, mainly because of the storage capability using bottles. When it comes to motion, the applications are rather limited. Vehicles can, of course, be gas-powered and large industrial motion can be accomplished with gas, though Diesel is more suitable. But imagine having your food blender or a desk fan run on gas! Electricity makes it a lot easier to accomplish motion applications. Even lighting can be done with less waste heat and thus more efficiently. The fact that gas needs oxygen for the combustion process is an issue in most indoor applications, anyhow. So is the waste heat. But the vast majority of electricity applications cannot be reasonably realized with gas. Think of entertainment and information systems, such as TV sets and personal computers. Or dishwashers, washing machines, telephones, doorbells, alarm and surveillance systems. Or the entire area of automation, which we will talk a lot more about in the next chapters. The breadth of applications possible and the ease of utilizing electrical power for them is what gave Electrification its enormous tailwind and ensured proliferation. Proliferation again drove adoption and growth, scale and thus lower cost.

On top of this, electricity is highly standardized, which beats other primary fuels, such as coal, oil, wood, and other primary renewable sources - even gas. Those come in ever-changing properties and they differ regionally. This standardization is what amplifies the second driver for the success of electricity: it is easy to make products that use it. Never in the history of technological innovation has one enabler stirred such a flurry of new ideas and inventions. In principle, any commercial or residential building serves also as the energy system into which applications can just be plugged in. That makes it possible to leave that part out of the product since the product designer can rely on the ubiquitous provision of that part of the overall product functionality. The interface between the building and the product is simply the wall socket, which provides heavily defined and quality ensured energy. And in this standardization and quality lies also the third and final differentiator of electricity. While accidents happen, and electricity as a form of energy, of course, has the potential to harm, the broad proliferation made it possible to develop the necessary protection technology along with the products that make and use electricity. A substantial part of the overall electricity system is devoted to safety and security, the closer it is to the end users. This applies even more so when it comes to investments in R&D. The entire protection relay system and control system on the network level, as well as the fuses and circuit breakers in the fuse box at home, are dedicated to safety. A third of all wires and cables are protective in nature.

An application that benefited perhaps more than most others from these specific capabilities of electrical systems is the computer. It needs moderate amounts of energy that are available in every building, it is sensitive to disruptions, and its circuits use electricity for signal processing. Computers only became possible due to electricity, and they also furthered the proliferation of electricity because every institution, every business, and eventually every household need them. As it was in the very beginning, with the telegraph being the first application for electricity, it was a technology from the Realm of Automation that cemented the towering position of Electrification as one of the most important achievements of mankind. Electrification also demonstrated the power of networked systems and the network effect of a dominant standard in business models.

There is a flip side of the coin, though. Industrialization, during the first phase, created substantial problems for the working class, and the focus on maximizing output led to pollution, issues with public health, and overstretch of natural resources, while Electrification nourished an enormous hunger for energy. Due to the availability of fossil fuels in seemingly infinite amounts, economies pressed forward with energy-intensive processes and industries, without looking at potential consequences. While electrical motion applications reduced pollution at the workplaces, the large-scale thermal generation needed for it let emissions skyrocket and grew the CO_2 footprint of humankind significantly. The focus of the future will be on sustainably deriving electricity. But during the first half of the 20th century, waste and pollution-intensive industry and CO_2-producing power generation accelerated. Electrification can almost be seen as an amplifier of the environmental issues of Industrialization.

On the other hand, Electrification demanded, for the first time, to have control systems that spanned entire countries, with millions of assets within integrated networks, being supervised, protected, and controlled. This intrinsic need for information management and control furthered what would be the core of the Third Industrial Revolution. This happened in the Realm of Automation, taking what was possible to the next level; a level of remote control and complex, automatic work orders where entire work processes can be implemented with automated machines. We call this kind of system a robot.

CHAPTER NINE

Robotization

The Third Realm of Innovation started with traps, the first automata. Ever since, managing time has been an intrinsic element of progress in this realm. Automation gave time back to the human species and will eventually allow us to return to a healthy level of around 20 hours of work per week or less. That does, of course, not exclude the possibility of spending this additional time in meaningful ways. On the contrary, a lot of what we can then do might be more significant than what we do today.

Through the centuries, the focus of innovators in the Automation realm has been very much on timekeeping itself. The aspect of time-saving, at the core of the original kickstarter, the traps, only came back with the Third Industrial Revolution. In between, most of the useful applications were around clocks, while from time to time curiosities were presented, often by clockmakers. Dolls that moved and were able to write a predefined sentence, mechanical animals displaying some movements. Clockmakers were interested to not only provide means to measure time but also to predict astrological events and to help with navigation. That demanded computational abilities. Several mechanical aids for arithmetic operations have been found, dating back to 2400 BCE. First, more complex mechanical computers were astrolabes used around 200 BCE by the Greeks. Innovators in Persia and Arabia improved those further during the medieval time frame. The slide rule was added at the beginning of the 17th century.

All these devices served as reckoning machines. They were not universal in nature and were not automatic in terms of operation. That only changed in 1833 with Charles Babbage's Analytical Engine. Babbage made use of an idea from the Industrial Revolution: punched cards. Those were used to control Jacquard looms, to create weaving patterns. He used such cards to feed information, both programs and data, to the machine. The computer itself consisted of that reader, a logic unit, a control unit, memory, and an output mechanism.

The design was so demanding in terms of fabrication of the parts, that the British Government stopped the funding eventually, since manually making the necessary thousands of parts was too time-consuming. Babbage was so far ahead that people around him lacked the imagination required to follow his passion and to be patient enough. He never completed the machine, but in 1888 his son Henry presented a simpler version, which was later used to calculate tables.

Mechanization provided the machines, manufacturing capabilities, and tools, and Electrification added the versatile energy to serve as the foundation for the Third Industrial Revolution. Machine tools and production machines had so successfully been mechanically automated that businesses demanded more. They required automation not only in a fixed, single-purpose way but flexibly and dynamically. Flexible meant that automation was not only able to conduct one task, but could be programmed to perform different tasks. That is the next level in Automation, and we call machines like this robot. Like with Electrification, the first actual elements in the Robotization space focused on Informatization. In Electrification it was the telegraph, in Robotization, the computer.

Let us quickly talk about the word robot. It means laborer, in the sense of a machine that can be forced to do work. The image in our heads is often influenced by science fiction literature and movies that show humanoid machines that conduct tasks by mimicking human behavior. However, the critical differentiator of a robot versus an automatic engine of any kind is that robots are flexible. A robot must be able to conduct different tasks, as programmed. For that, it does not need to be humanoid at all. Almost all robots existing today are not.

Moreover, it does not necessarily need to be able to move around. Again most robots today are stationary. Often, there is not even a need for a mechanical aspect at all, although most robots have motion capabilities, and industrial robots typically have a mechanical arm. A robot can also be an interactive machine with a screen, input and output systems, and an operating system that allows running different programs. So that is precisely what a computer is. We recognize that computers, especially the PC or Personal Computer, and its successors like tablet computers and smartphones, are the core enabler of Digitalization, the Fourth Industrial Revolution. However, the computer itself is Automation. The software running on it has evolved into the core of Digitalization, although the origin of using computers was a lot more modest. Indeed, directly or remotely steering mechanical machines was, from the get-go, an essential task for computers.

Computers started as huge machines, filling entire rooms, consuming significant amounts of energy, and indeed containing a lot of electromechanical devices. The access to such technology was regulated, and the hurdles to owning such a computer were significant. Only governments, large corporations, and pioneering universities had the means, and thus defined the applications. Those were mainly in areas such as data crunching for statistical processes, or fast computations of relatively simple functions using – for the time – the groundbreaking speed of the computers. Automating the calculations necessary to guide a torpedo towards a hit on a moving target is a classic example. The amount of code for such a calculation is tiny, the input data set as well. The output data is again just a small set of numbers. What made these calculation robots so valuable was the very little time it took between the input of that small dataset to see the output result. Saving time meant acting faster, having outcomes before others could have them. For military applications, it meant to hit before being hit.

Computers taking off

Computers, at the beginning, were not perceived as a technology that would gain broad adoption. The machines were too large, too expensive, and the concept was to have all computing power centralized. In the 1940s to '60s, that was the mantra and it led to a belief that broader access for users would work only with allotted access time, or timeslices, on even more massive, central computers. The alleged statement of former IBM chairman Thomas Watson, "I see a nationwide market of perhaps five computers" exemplifies this thinking, although he might never have meant that the market would stay like that. IBM evolved from CTR, Computing-Tabulating-Recording Company, which itself was a merger of four companies.

First and foremost was the Hollerith Company, founded by Herman Hollerith in 1896. Already during the national US census of 1880 and 1890 his tabulating machines had been used in a direct contract with the Census Office. The growing population and the more massive requested sets of data meant an ever-growing effort not only for the enumeration itself but also for the creation of a host of reports for different purposes. The tabulating machines used punched cards and electromagnetic sensors that could detect if there was a hole at a specific place of the card or not, and for counting purposes that created an electric signal that drove a counting dial. Alexander Dey introduced the dial recorder in 1888. This counting machine looked like a big clock and counted the work hours of employees by tracking the arrival and exit times. Smaller versions were designed to track up to 50 workers, while large versions managed 200 employees. Dey and his brother founded the company in Syracuse, New York, while still residing in Scotland. American inventor Willard Bundy presented similar products, and the Bundy Manufacturing Company became a kind of category killer in time recorders, which at the time were often referred to as "Bundies" by the workforce. Another forerunner was Julius Pitrap's computing scale. The first version, patented in 1885, computed the sales price of a product while measuring the weight. A later version was able to compound several such weighing operations. A classical application was in retail, where different products with different prices per pound could be weighed out, and the total bill for the customer resulted in the end. His activities were acquired by the International Time Recording Company. These four enterprises were the core of CTR. Their products were machines, but not so much for the factory as for the office environment. They drove productivity in areas such as accounting, compiling reports, and generating payrolls. The term business machines described this new market. CTR consequently rebranded itself as International Business Machines or short IBM in 1924.

Another area of interest for business automation at the time was in the area of cash registration in retail and especially hospitality businesses. Patrons in restaurants and bars would pay cash, but not all of that money ended up in the cash drawer of the business owner. James Ritty, like Pitrap from Ohio, was a saloon operator and had a brother, John, who was a mechanic. Ritty wanted to solve the issue of "corrupt" cash registering and came up with the first mechanical cash register. He filed for a patent in 1879. His product was a success and was soon improved with a locked cash drawer, which only opened when the total key was pressed and at the same time chimed a bell to alert the shop owner that a transaction was happening. Ritty's heart was in the hospitality business though. He preferred to open a second bar instead of focusing on his small manufacturing company, which he sold to a group of investors, among those the Patterson brothers – John and Frank. In 1884 the brothers rebranded Ritty's company as National Cash Register Company, or NCR for short. John Henry Patterson created with NCR the first progressive, modern American company. Unlike the dark and gloomy manufacturing halls of the First Industrial Revolution, his vision was light-flooded factories with entire walls made of glass. He put a considerable emphasis on workers' welfare. He established the first company-own sales training center in 1893 and established a modern sales culture. The whole idea of having the sales force treated as a unique asset that needed to be taken care of and groomed was revolutionary at the time. Patterson and his team came up with many sales tactics that became part of the repertoire of any successful B2B marketing. It is a curious fact of history that one quite innovative employee, who worked his way up from a failed butcher shop owner to the general sales manager of NCR, was fired by Patterson in 1914. He left to join CTR and became the iconic, long-term chairman of IBM: Thomas J. Watson.

Back to IBM. With the addition of an electric motor to the NCR cash registers by Charles F. Kettering in 1906, the Electrification of business machines began. That opened a host of new opportunities for business machines to become more complex and powerful. In 1933 IBM introduced its Type 285 electric bookkeeping and accounting machine: a tabulator with an integrated (numeric) printer. The machine processed more than two punched cards per second. Alphanumeric printing, gang punching, and summary punching featured in the series 400 and 500 machines. The last of those were still on the market in 1975. However, in 1946, IBM introduced the first-ever electronic multiplier.

Multiplication had been achieved electromechanically before, but the speed was slow, and the card feeding and subsequent punching of the answer had to follow after an interruption, often lasting for several cycles. With the IBM 603, the answer was computed so fast and fed back via cables to the card processing unit that no interruption was needed. The calculation speed was several orders of magnitude faster than before and accomplished with electronic tubes. It multiplied six-digit factors. The equipment was still somewhat bulky and the tubes needed much power. That would change almost ten years later with the 608, which used transistors and magnetic core memory. The footprint of the machine was 50% smaller and the power consumption a staggering 90% lower, while computation speeds were so fast that a nine-digit multiplication completed 4'400 times faster than the card puncher was able to actually punch the result. The magnetic core memory stored information indefinitely, also with the power switched off. This step illustrates a fundamental concept of Automation, to drive the needed resources - in this case, space and electric power - down while allowing increased automatic completion of more sophisticated tasks. More importantly, the 608 introduced what real computers needed: fast-acting memory and the ability to perform all basic arithmetic operations in one machine. The business machines before were specialized. Addition and subtraction needed one type, multiplication another, and the same for the even slower division operations. Compiling for summary printing was again another machine, and so forth. With the 610, which can be called the first ever Personal Computer, all tasks could be done in one machine, consisting of memory, control unit, paper tape reader and puncher, an alphanumeric printer, and an operator keyboard. The latter featured a small cathode-ray tube screen that allowed the operator to look at the content of any of the memory registers. The machine was broadly and flexibly used for scientific computations, actuarial calculations, solving polynomial equations, integration of differential equations, and any other operation that could fit into the 2'604 digits of addressable memory. Allowing a user to conceive a program to solve a particular problem, like a statistical analysis operation, entering it into the machine as an instruction set and then run the machine to perform a task, or even an infinite series of calculations based on a data feed, made the 610 a real, flexible automation system. IBM sold some 180 units. By the way, most customers leased the machines, which was standard for business machines at the time.

Commercial users started to embrace the possibilities this new technology would offer. Their approach was not, of course, to have several individual users to program, enter data, and operate the computer, like a scientist in a research lab would do it. They had large departments dealing with accounting, bank transactions, and human-resource-related operations. Being able to handle say five times as many transactions with the same amount of people was a meaningful target. For that, not all members of such a department had to be on the same level. Some operated the computer equipment, consisting of a wall of cabinets or frames that contained memory, CPU's, and control units, and hosts of printers and data readers. Another small team dealt with programming the computers, creating, in principle, company propriety software that fulfilled internal specifications. The majority were busy feeding data, collecting paper-based data, handling printed reports, and so on. The main property of such systems was scalability, which made it possible to process a certain amount of transactions within a shift, for example, to settle all accounts before a mandatory cutoff time. By adding the respective number of units and the right mix of personnel, companies or government agencies were able to cope with the growth in data processing demands. This kind of computer – centralized, scalable, and made for a determined number crunching task – was referred to as mainframe computer. The term references the large cabinets or frames housing the processing units.

By the end of the 1950s, the mainframe became the poster child of data crunching. Especially IBM's 7000 series and later the 360 series dominated the market. In the first two decades, the US market, which was leading the adoption of mainframe computing, was served by what people called "IBM and the Seven Dwarfs." With IBM's market share dwarfing that of the other competitors combined, IBM was able to call the shots. The Seven Dwarfs were Burroughs, NCR, Control Data Corporation, UNIVAC, Honeywell, GE, and RCA. After some consolidation at the beginning of the seventies, what was left called itself the BUNCH, which stood for the starting letters of Burroughs, UNIVAC, NCR, Control Data Corporation, and Honeywell. Those manufacturers all followed IBM into the next phase, the era of mini– and then microcomputers.

Minicomputers became possible with the reduced footprint of transistorized computers and magnetic core memory, and were meant to serve a client base that didn't need the massive scalability of mainframes for recordkeeping and transaction processing. They instead needed computational power for a particular task, such as the upcoming Computer-Aided Design or CAD of the 1970's. Minicomputers were often sold to OEM's who used them to control their sophisticated equipment, such as laboratory equipment, telecoms switching systems and similar differentiated tasks. The company that became almost synonymous with the minicomputer was Digital Equipment Corporation or short DEC. Their approach was to have a Complex Instruction Set Computer - or CISC - based on their proprietary Instruction Set Architecture (ISA). That was first the Programmed Data Processor ISA or PDP and later the iconic VAX ISA. VAX stood for Virtual Address Extension, which allowed the application of so-called virtual memory to allow addressing a larger address space. The instruction set was programmer friendly, and that was important for smaller companies that wanted to customize the VAX for their OEM solutions. The size of the minicomputers was more like that of a fridge, instead of a room-filling mainframe. That made it easier to transport and install minicomputers as part of an instrumentation or control application in industrial plants as well. DEC evolved to become the second largest computer manufacturer behind

IBM and became the epitome of minicomputers. In the 20 years up to 1985, around 100 minicomputer manufacturers sprang up. Less than ten lasted and only a handful survived the coming onslaught of the microcomputers. While the business machines had many roots in Ohio, and the mainframes had been a New York-driven endeavor, the minicomputer firms were mainly in the New England states. When the minicomputers were squashed between the mainframe and the microcomputer world, it shook the high-tech industry in Massachusetts to such a degree that the entire state fell into decline. The decline of the "Massachusetts Miracle" at the end of the 1980s hit companies such as DEC, Prime, Wang Labs, Lotus, and others.

The era that followed, with microcomputers becoming a household item, would later set the scene for the Fourth Industrial Revolution: Digitalization.

The Microcomputer

Before we discuss microcomputers, let us quickly clarify what supercomputers are since those are on the other side of the spectrum. First of all, they are not mainframes.

Mainframes are built for scaling up, to be reliable in 24-hour operations throughout the year, and are optimized for recordkeeping and relatively simple types of calculations. Supercomputers, on the other hand, are tuned for maximum computing power. In the early 1950s, science and mathematics research presented several challenges that needed massive computing power, and companies such as Engineering Research Associates (ERA) specialized in building machines for example for code breaking for the military. One of the genius engineers at ERA was young Seymour Cray. His ambition to drive what was then called scientific computing to the next level made him leave ERA and found his own company Control Data Corporation, together with William Norris. They developed the first commercial supercomputer, the CDC 6600. Cray understood that for supercomputing, scale and sheer processor power was not the only route to go. Managing the process of getting data into and out of the CPU, the so-called I/O handling, was as important as the CPU clock speed. He made sure that the processors received enough data to crunch, reducing idle time. He also balanced the entire system to make sure that the different parts worked smoothly together. Other companies attempting to outpace the Cray machines were not as successful. At the same time, CDC maintained focus on cost. Cray's opinion was that customers should expect to get four times the performance when they were willing to pay double the price. The next generation, the CDC 7600, had ten times the performance and cemented CDC's and Cray's nimbus of the cradle of supercomputing. His relentless focus on making the fastest computer on Earth made him again leave and found Cray Research and later Cray Computer Corporation. He stuck with his mantra that every new generation of a product should have ten times the performance of the predecessor. This development allowed scientists to solve ever-larger optimization problems, run simulations, and interpret massive amounts of data in areas such as nuclear physics. The Cold War was the fuel to get the funding for the increasing cost of such massive computing power. The current and final frontier for supercomputing is the simulation of the entire global weather, with a forecasting capability of two weeks. For that Erik DeBenedictis of Sandia National Labs, one of the foremost supercomputing users, estimates that a so-called zettaFLOPS computer would be needed, a computer that could run a sextillion FLOPS or floating-point operations per second. That is ten to the power of twenty-one. FLOPS are the kph of computing, a way to describe the speed of a computer. Such performance might be possible by 2030. Today's fastest machines manage exaFLOPS, which is 1'000 times less. Such a computer already consumes 500 MW of power. Imagine the electricity bill.

One thing that supercomputers had in common with the upcoming microcomputer world in the early seventies was the focus on system optimization and cost-effectiveness. That allowed getting performance for the money. In supercomputing that meant getting a massive performance for a given, though sizable, budget. In microcomputing, this meant making computers available to users with quite restricted budgets. In the early seventies, nerds and engineers thirsted for access to a computer. Universities, school labs, and engineering departments of smaller firms all wanted to become part of this new and exciting time. However, mainframes and even minicomputers were unaffordable. The intricate architecture of such machines made it difficult to produce them in garage operations for tinkerers or in a mass-production mode for the consumer market. That changed when the first microprocessors entered the market. Microprocessors had the complete functionality of whole racks of circuit boards, miniaturized and integrated into one large-scale circuit on a semiconductor base. That made the processor much smaller, more resilient and reliable and with lower production costs. That was precisely what an appliance needed if ordinary people were to afford and operate it.

Similarly, microcomputers used semiconductor memory instead of the cumbersome magnetic core memory boards. The company that became the front-runner of this technology and would remain one of the pillars of the entire microcomputer and personal computer boom was Intel. So it was an Intel 8008 chip that powered the world's first microcomputer, the Micral N, early in 1973. It was the first commercially available, solid-state computer, using a microprocessor and semiconductor memory. French company R2E developed the machine for the Institut National de la Recherche Agronomique, which asked for a low-cost process control computer for its research activities, instead of using PDP based minicomputers. The Micral used punched tape for programming. Later that year an 8-inch floppy disk reader was added. The Micral was around five times cheaper than a small minicomputer. A year later the SCELBI entered the North American market, also based on Intel 8008. But compared to the around 90'000 units sold by R2E over the years, SCELBI Computer Consulting sold less than 200. In 1975 the US market woke up to the Altair 8800, which made use of the Intel 8080 chip. The company that developed it was MITS (Micro Instrumentation and Telemetry Systems).

MITS had been active since 1969 making desktop calculators. When that market became brutally competitive, the company smartly entered a new niche. MITS was surprised when they sold thousands of kits in the first month alone.

Everything happened so fast that MITS did not even have a proper name for the product. They asked Popular Electronics magazine editor Les Solomon to come up with a name before putting the product on the title of his magazine. Lore has it that Les' daughter Lauren proposed Altair since that was the Enterprise's destination on that night's Star Trek episode. Another last-minute effort was the BASIC programming language for the Altair. MITS-founder Ed Roberts had been contacted by a company called Traf-O-Data to ask if MITS wanted to use their BASIC compiler. Traf-O-Data did not have a BASIC for an 8080 based system yet. They were merely testing the water. Once Roberts confirmed his interest, two gentlemen started to work on the compiler: Bill Gates and Paul Allen. They had about a month before their bluff would be called and they worked day and night on a minicomputer running an 8080 simulator. Once the software was complete, Paul Allen flew to New Mexico to deliver Altair-BASIC to MITS on a paper tape. This par force effort laid the foundation for a company that would play a role as important as Intel's in the microcomputer world: Microsoft.

Robots conquering the factories

What is the first thought when we look at automation in the industrial space and especially Robotization? For many of us, the first image that comes to mind is one of the impressive body-in-white production lines, where hosts of industrial robots use their six-axis arms mounted with welding guns to assemble car bodies for the automotive industry. And indeed, it is a powerful depiction of the impact and meaning of Robotization. Like an awe-inspiring ballet, dancing to a choreography of logic and optimization, the robots move in perfect harmony, with sparks from the spot welding action flying every couple of seconds. The automotive industry is still the more extensive industry user of industrial robots. For car manufacturing plants, welding is also always the most essential robotized activity when counting the number of installed units. At the same time, applications are very diversified, from machine tending to paint lines, application of glues and sealants, deburring of parts, and gearbox assembly. The introduction of collaborative robots, or cobots, which can work right next to humans will further grow the application space, especially in the assembly sphere. Cobots do not need to be installed in a

163

caged safety zone. Their sensors help them avoid colliding with or hurting humans.

Meanwhile, usage outside of the automotive sector is multiplying, both in unit count and breadth of applications. General manufacturing activities in areas like plastic injection molding, tool and machine tending, and activities such as coating, painting, and even 3D printing make use of robots. A considerable area of use is the handling of semi-finished goods in the production of semiconductors, solar panels, batteries for electric mobility, and flatscreens. In all these cases, the careful transfer, the cleanroom compliance, and the high precision are arguments for the use of robots. A similar effect is visible in the production of food and beverages. The absence of humans in many picking and packaging activities for perishable food items allows robots to work in extremely cold or hot environments and also ensures very high levels of hygiene. That permits extending the shelf life of the end product while reducing scrap rates during production as well, thus helping to cut back on food waste. The eBusiness boom of the last decades made warehouse operations even more critical. Modern, fully automatic warehouse operations use very high degrees of Robotization, from inbound to outbound operations as well as the composition of packaging for individual order fulfillment.

Automated Guided Vehicles, or AGVs, move containers and crates around, shelf stackers store away products, and palletizing robots stack boxes onto pallets for transport. The computer system that allows fully automatic warehouse operations is the only way to know where which product is stored; systems like this need to function with utmost reliability. Just imagine if a large distribution warehouse, with millions of items scattered across hundreds of thousands of stock-keeping units, would all of a sudden lose its full status control and require a manual audit to regain control. The interruption of service would be costly and an embarrassment for the logistics process.

The critical success factor for industrial robots and the collateral machinery for Robotization around them has never been the replacement of human labor for cost reasons. Rather, assurance of quality, avoidance of scrap, increased energy efficiency, and taking humans out of dull, dangerous, and dirty activities have been the driving factors. Only recently, with changes in demographics, the lack of available workforce in industrialized countries has become a factor as well.

We already mentioned that the control system in a robotized warehouse is mission- critical. That brings us to the other significant - but less visible - use of Robotization in the industrial world: the control of production processes. Indeed, one of the first use cases for computers was plant control. Especially the minicomputer size of earlier times was used for the control of complex OEM machinery and control of production processes. We can distinguish between discreet production processes using Programmable Logic Controllers, or PLC, and continuous production processes that more often use Distributed Control Systems, or DCS. In a discreet or factory automation case, the product moves from station to discrete station and could be picked up in between, for example, for inspection. The process is cycled but can be halted without damaging the product.

A good example is classical assembly lines where, at every station, one or several additions or modifications happen before the product moves, for instance, on a conveyor belt, to the next person or robot. That allows island automation, with islands along the line simply moving products and communicating a simple stop-and-go signal to its neighbors. Within an island, the automation tasks are often quite demanding and need high-speed computing. The number of signals that the controller can receive or send - the so-called input/output channels, or I/O - is rather limited since only sensors and actuators of that one island are inside the system. Machinery islands often have 300 to 500 I/O.

On the other end of the I/O scale are continuous production plants. They are typical for process industries. Here the product is made in a process that either runs continuously for as long as possible or it runs during the production of a batch. The product cannot be taken out of the process, which must not be halted. A production halt usually leads to the loss of an entire batch, or needs laborious cleaning and restarting of the process machinery.

A good example is the process of papermaking. The paper machine, a 300m long colossus with hundreds of rollers, belts, meshes, reels, and winders, works - in a modern machine - with 1'800m per minute, shooting out a 10m wide web of paper for winding on the master roller at the end of the paper machine. The input on the wet end is pulp slurry, which throughout the process is shaped, pressed, dried, smoothed, and trimmed until it reaches the dry end side of the machine. Around 2'000 motors driving the rotational elements in the machine need to all be finely synchronized to prevent the ripping of the paper web. Each web break costs around an hour of production, or a million sqm of paper, and means tediously restarting the process. Imagine a group of people holding the unwound content of a roll of toilet paper, doused with water, running with that long stretch of delicate matter in one direction, with such a perfectly controlled speed that the dripping, mushy paper never rips. Now imagine doing this with over 100 kilometers per hour speed, for 24 hours straight. And that is just the speed drive control task of the system. Additionally, the system needs to apply heated air, spray water, precisely heat the rollers, and move mechanical actuators. To be able to optimize the process, the system receives terabytes of data every hour from arrays of sensors and cameras. It scans every inch of the paper at different stages of the production process. By using high-speed computers, the machine analyzes every bit of sensor input to predict the quality of the product and to inform decisions to make tiny control changes to keep the paper within a tight quality band. Such a paper mill has perhaps 10'000 I/O channels as well as camera feeds, which are also utilized for control purposes. Other examples of process industries using DCS are chemical, petrochemical, steel making, and minerals processing plants.

A broad product range needs a bit of both a continuous or batch process to make the base product and factory automation to package it. Pharmaceutical products are an excellent example of such hybrid industries. The active pharmaceutical ingredient is made in a large-scale batch process. The end result of that is the feedstock for a filling plant or a tablet press with blister packaging and cartoning.

In these processes, islands are often PLC controlled, with master control of the entire discreet end of production being managed by the DCS as a manufacturing execution system.

Plant control systems have made significant progress over the decades since the earliest applications in the 1950s. A useful way to measure that progress is to look at the number of I/O supervised by one human in the loop. Take a typical control-intensive industry, like conventional power generation. Before digital control systems were introduced, a single operator in the control room of a power plant handled less than 300, often even as little as 100, I/O channels. All instruments showed direct, unfiltered values and were sometimes placed, almost arbitrarily, wherever there was space on the control board. No pre-computing. The operator had to interpret - so to speak - naked data coming from the process, in a variety of measurement units and scales. Whether the process was under control depended on the abilities of the operator and the team members to understand and "feel" the process in real time.

As soon as the first control systems were introduced, a key advantage was that groups of logically connected signals could also be displayed next to each other. Information could be enhanced, for example, with color coding. Showing critical values in alarm colors, or instrument readouts flashing, would attract the operator's attention. The computer was used to pre-analyze the data input, compute averages, and store and display time series, or composite units. The number of I/O per operator jumped by a factor of ten, while the control capabilities exploded, allowing for more efficient operations. In the 1980s, the user interfaces were further improved, replacing control panels and mosaic displays with computer screens, now also allowing animated representations of the process.

Step by step, the ergonomic aspects of the operator workplace, the overall control room environment, and especially the way the graphical user interfaces (GUI) was designed allowed the running of more complex operations with less personnel. Today, a single operator can handle over 30'000 I/O channels, while adding numerous additional tasks like alarm handling, service and maintenance dispatching, and continuous process tuning. One of the critical enablers for this is so-called high-performance user interfaces. That term does not refer to the screen resolution, even though the operator desks today have far superior monitors. The term refers to the aim of the user interface to make the users, or operators, high performing. For example, not-so-relevant information is shaded in lighter gray colors or even blurred slightly, emphasizing those parts of the information that at this point are of interest. Certainly, color is used a lot less offensively than in the 1990s, when control system interfaces had an almost psychedelic appearance, with vendors proudly demonstrating the color abilities of their systems. The trend is towards GUIs that show more and more consolidated and pre-interpreted data. Instead of showing a long time series of data points for the controlled temperature of a reactor, a simple traffic light shows 'green' as long as the temperature stays within the defined band. Once the control system detects a trend pointing to the value`s potential to move out of the band, the traffic light turns yellow by applying predictive data analytics and a host of context information shows up next to it. The operator only jumps to action when and where needed and in such a case, is armed with the necessary conclusive data to make decisions.

In the case of alarms, the system studies in the background how and when alarms come to exist and with which other factors they correlate. An alarm is a message to the operator that something is wrong in a part of the plant, for example, with one of the assets. Let us say the operator gets an alarm for a blender motor in the North part of the plant. It is a vibration alarm. Curiously the blender is not even running. That has happened several times during the last days. The operator frowns but does not really have an explanation. At the same time in the control room of the plant utilities, the operator sees the tripping of an electric power circuit, wonders why that happens, and takes actions to mitigate the effect by switching loads and restoring power.

The control system uses its data access to run analytics on this alarm, establishing that this kind of warning occurs three minutes after a pump in the South part of the plant is activated. This feed water pump is quite essential, and it is good that it works. So far, this all looks unrelated. The system runs correlations with processes that also take three minutes and finds a number of those. For example, the back-up diesel in the North area needs three minutes to start up from idle mode. The control system might not understand why, but it just found the root cause for the vibration alarm. Each time the large feed water pump starts, it overloads the electric circuit, which trips. The back-up diesel generators kick in action to make the critical pump work. Their vibration is transferred to the blender motor's bearing vibration sensor. Despite the blender not running, this is exciting news. The root cause analysis leads to hooking up the heavy-duty pump to a separate electric feeder, avoiding the trips, avoiding the start of the diesel generator, avoiding the vibration, thus, no alarm anymore. Without a control system, this kind of situation would perhaps have slipped the operator's attention, and even if it had not, it would have been challenging to connect the dots.

Robotization does what Automation has always done. It gives us back time. Time to be creative, cultivate new ideas, further optimize processes, and improve our products. Robotization is so far the most potent instrument to drive resource and energy efficiency. It helps us to make up for the negative impact that Industrialization and early Electrification had on our planet. It helps us to do what we do in a better way, in a more sophisticated and sustainable way.

An explosion of applications

Robotization does not remain inside the offices or stop at the factory gates. Once the critical mass of technologies, components, and applications was in existence, the consumer market picked up the promises of this new era. With the microcomputer and the PC being introduced first on the university level, then on the school level, a new generation of computer-savvy people dreamed of having a computer at home. Learning to program a computer and using standard software packages became a part of education and for many, a hobby. Household appliances were electrified already in the 1930s, which was the precondition for Automation.

Already in 1937 Bendix Home Appliances introduced the first automatic washing machine, although this was mainly used in public laundromats. Only after World War II did automatic appliances start to gain global traction. The design included quite intricate electromechanical timers driven by miniature electric motors. It is hard to believe, but this timer was the most expensive part of the entire machine. Today's appliances are often entirely robotized. That means, they are flexible with a variety of programs, can react to measurement values, optimize water and power consumption, or use tariff advantages like cheaper night power. Washing machines measure how dirty a load of laundry is and what the weight of the clothes is. That allows the device to plan the best washing procedure and dosage of detergent. Dishwashers work similarly. One of the latest appliance categories to become robotized is vacuum cleaners. And since they are not just sitting in the laundry room or the kitchen aisle humming a bit while doing their work, their movement around the house fascinates consumers.

The autonomous movement plays a role in transport as well. What started with unmanned aerial vehicles for the military, also known as drones, has become a versatile technology used for commercial transportation, recreational purposes, for pipeline inspection, science, and agricultural applications. The autonomous flight operation allows drones to be way lighter than vehicles that need to carry and support a human pilot. That and the optimization of robotized flight will enable drones to stay in the air for an extended period. Drones can be fully autonomous or remote-controlled. But remote control does not mean that they are remotely flown. They merely receive indicative directions but still conduct the flight maneuvers on their own.

Once the fundamental principles and algorithms had been perfected for military or professional use cases, the consumer market drove up the unit count of drones into the millions, imposing a steep learning curve. With every duplication of the cumulative production of drones, the unit cost goes down by around 30%. That in turn makes drones affordable for the next lower market segment. In Robotization, as in Automation in general, we often observe this effect. Once the consumer market, with its vast unit counts, kicks in and fuels the learning curve, the development of technology accelerates enormously — both functionality and cost – and benefits from step-change improvement. There is no reason to believe that marine vessels and automotive applications would not become autonomous within the next decades. The advantages are simply mind-boggling. Robotized vehicles will drive down the number of accidents, can harmonize traffic flow with swarm behavior, and do not need to park in densely populated areas. But the biggest gain in terms of economic impact is that we will not waste time steering a car. In 2016, American drivers were found to spend, on average, 17'600 minutes behind the steering wheel per year. That is 5% of the awake hours. Or 16% of the total work hours. Once we all use autonomous transport pods, if not even virtual reality systems, we will think back and ask ourselves how we were able to tolerate such a time waste.

An area that will see a massive advent of robotics is the service area: both humanoid robots that can support applications in human care because they blend in, and robots where form follows function, supporting service activities in areas such as food preparation. Humanoid robots fill a gap caused by labor markets or demographics. Aging populations and populations affluent enough to maintain not only life but also health are putting a strain on the care sector that can hardly be tackled with care personnel from younger generations alone. Once the demography of a nation starts to normalize - meaning the flat pyramid-shaped distribution that we see in rapidly developing countries moves towards the roughly rectangular distribution that our species had for hundreds of thousands of years - the transition is a difficult period to manage. While the result, the rectangular distribution, means that each age cohort is roughly the same size, it does take many generations to again arrive at that stage. But from where does the pyramidal distribution stem? Anthropologists and demographical simulations hint that until around 10'000 BCE, life-extending progress was slow enough not to modify the age distribution. One could say the rectangular distribution chart just slowly grew in height, representing a slightly higher average age at death. Humans reached an average age of around 20 to 25 years. Enough to create offspring and help the children to learn the basics of self-sustaining. Life span in many species seems to be limited by the ability to find or generate enough food. That is called caloric restriction. If individuals of a species have access to significantly more than the minimum amount of food, their life span doubles. That is what happened with humankind during the First Agricultural Revolution, starting in the Fertile Crescent around 10'000 BCE.

The ability to farm and to store food reserves, adding to the gathering and hunting abilities, allowed the species to extend its expected life span at birth to around 30 years. That is where it hovered for thousands of years, until a dramatic inflection point around 1870. When Industrialization fueled the Second Agricultural Revolution – as discussed in the chapter on the First Industrial Revolution – with modernized equipment and ways to increase yield rates, the life expectancy started to rise rapidly as well. Beginning in Europe, the Americas, and Oceania, the value shot up to 70 years within one century. In Asia and finally Africa, the trend started in the early part of the 20th century. Compared to the first round adding ten years over the course of a millennium, adding 40 years over the course of a tenth of the time was dramatic. It allowed massive proliferation and high population growth.

The resulting age distribution was skewed significantly towards young people. In most of our school textbooks, this population pyramid is taught as the healthy or 'normal' case. But in reality, it is an exceptional case. The motivation for families to have so many children was based on two things: it was now possible, due to the availability of food, and the growing life expectancy made parents think about their retirement. Retirement must have been a meaningless word before 1870. People worked, had several children, most of whom died, then parents themselves worked until they died at about 30 years. Well, 30 years is an average, statistically expected value. There was an occasional old-timer reaching 50 or 60 years. Those people indeed needed help and sustenance from the younger generation. But that put little strain on the population. Once the age outlook exploded, people became wary about getting older and their children were their 'social insurance'.

Fortunately, we know that once a national economy reaches a certain level of wealth or economic power, this behavior changes. In literature we often find statistics showing that an annual GDP of around 3'000 USD per head is the inflection point. Beyond that, proliferation rates drop rapidly towards a level of about two. That means each set of parents has around two children that survive until they reach their reproductive age. As you see, that will lead to a roughly rectangular age distribution again, like during most of the time humans have been roaming our planet. The issue is the transition between the two. When we follow a particular age cohort, say the generation born in the 1950s on a chart, we see that such a younger group moves upwards through the distribution chart, while medical progress extends the expected top of the chart. If that cohort is significantly larger than the following younger generations, it starts to look like a 'lump' in the chart, moving slowly to the top. For some time, the age distribution looks as if the famous pyramid was turned upside down. There are suddenly more older people than younger, a situation posing quite a challenge for several reasons. Besides, this situation is prolonged by the coinciding progress in life-extending technologies. The transition might well take a century. After that, things might well be back to 'normal,' and the world population will move towards its maximum point, asymptotically.

This unusual age distribution could have some adverse side effects if humankind is not smart enough to find solutions.

First of all, the ratio of economically active people vs. non-active becomes smaller. That could become a drag for overall national productivity. But experience shows that technological innovation can compensate for that by growing individual productivity. In the medical and care sector, we must not make an exception to that. With fewer and fewer young people available and the ratio to older and dependent people shrinking, productivity in this sector needs to grow rapidly. Having more robots on the factory floor is not too controversial, but robots taking care of the sick and elderly? That is a paradigm shift. Technologists need to step up their game and include more social science and user feedback into designing these products. Not only the individual patient but also society needs to cope with this change and be able to tolerate and accept the adjustment. To drive this, service robots in less contentious environments need to be introduced and urgently made normality. Robots that give guidance, or act as a receptionist, a host, deliver goods or perform other auxiliary tasks would be ideal.

Another area of concern is expertise. When the generation of today's 60-year-olds retires in highly developed countries, this means that the replacement is a smaller cohort. Additionally, the young generation might have other preferences and interests in terms of education. That could lead to an expertise chasm that needs to be bridged. We will come back to how Artificial Intelligence as part of Digitalization could help to overcome that gap.

But also, our political systems and value frameworks will come under stress. For the last 150 years, the time during which our current systems developed, youth always held the majority of voting rights. The large growing- up generations accelerated the modernization of societies; they helped with the introduction of new technologies, fueled the speed of innovation, and brought a sound future orientation into political decision-making. In the meantime, in ageing societies, democratic elections are won by whoever satisfies the wishes of the oldest generations. That puts a damper on the future orientation of political decision-making and legislation. The generation that has the least time to still spend on our planet decides what to do. The generations that will have to deal with the long-term effects of these decisions are the youngest — those who have the longest time to suffer the consequences still. In many democratically run countries, we can observe this. For example, short-term raises of pensions for retirees are put into action, depleting pension system reserves and displacing government investment. Tax cuts for mature salary earners are financed with huge public debt, which will not be paid back by those who benefit from it, but by future generations. There are different scenarios for how this could pan out. One thing is sure: going on as usual is not sustainable.

A driving factor for the fears that cause older generations to become conservative to the degree of being reactionary is that the costs of many things in their daily life are going up. Older people depend more on services than young people. Demographic change makes these services, like carers, hairdressers, skilled craftspeople, and similar much more expensive. Additionally, older people need more medical support and medication. That becomes more expensive over the span of their life because of higher individual needs. But also because life-prolonging, and health-prolonging medical technologies are subject to diminishing marginal returns. Each even-better pill, diagnostic technology, or surgical therapy is even more expensive and sophisticated than the one before. As a result, older people start to question whether they can maintain their standards. They start to be willing to sacrifice the future of their grandchildren for their own safety at the present time.

As technological innovators, we need to drive above-mentioned costs down. We need to demonstrate that we will be able to maintain living standards for senior citizens. Robotization in care, medical robots in surgery theaters, AI in diagnostics, service robots at home, personal electronic assistance systems can help to achieve this.

We cannot avoid touching upon an application sphere for Robotization that has always been a primary testbed for innovation: the military. As much as it frustrates us, conflict is still part of human nature. That also means that police forces and military forces are still needed to be able to tackle conflict potentials once diplomatic means have been exhausted. One of the highest costs for military interventions, besides the loss of life and health, is to maintain personnel on the battlefield and to transport personnel and the supplies related to it. Taking humans out of the battlefield and the combat vehicles reduces risks for them and drives the cost of operations down. Not being in personal danger might also allow more rational and commensurate decision-making. Having fewer troops directly involved in the horrors of combat reduces the amount of post-traumatic stress. In theory, a robot-supported fight should allow more precision, keeping collateral damage lower.

Given the above-mentioned demographic changes, wasting the life of young generations in combat cannot be an acceptable option. The more technologized battle becomes, the more it will be a function of the economic power of the combatants. Perhaps it has always been. Still, during the wars of the past, economic power meant the ability to draft large numbers of soldiers or slaves, to plunder supplies for troops en route, or to pay mercenary troops that often amplified atrocities.

Clearly, all of these arguments can have a dark side to them. Decision makers could face lower hurdles to start a war. Gamification of remote-controlled warfare might lower human barriers to kill. Societies without traumatized veterans might forget that war is a dark chapter in human civilization. And - as always with robots - people fear the uprise of the machines. Robots that kill, that are out of control. Societies will have to find ways to deal with those risks while continuing on the path we are on. Over the course of the last 70 years, measured in terms of combat activities per 100'000 world population, there has never been less war activity than today. The same applies to the number of casualties. Statistically, this trend is clearly there. Our perception might be different, driven by social media, omnipresent news, and the global reach of our ability to consume news. We need to work on making war and combat what it must be - a legitimized exception, based on the conviction that it is the lesser evil compared to the alternative non-intervention. An aspect that we often overlook is how the industrialized warfare, which humankind first experienced in World War I, is not only devastating to combatants but also the environment. Humans are wasteful and, when put into combat uniforms, this wastefulness multiplies. The argument that war justifies the means leads to the acceptance of ravaging the environment, leaving deadly poison, military supplies, and destroyed ecotopes behind. If robotized warfare helps cut the impact of war on our planet, it would be great progress. Nature and creation are not part of the conflict but suffer most.

CHAPTER TEN

What comes next in the first three Revolutions?

Before we speak about Digitalization, it makes sense to try and peek into the future of the first three realms. What happens there will have a profound impact on Digitalization. And the other way around. The first two Industrial Revolutions have been fantastic in terms of progress and have formed the foundation for humankind's future. But they also placed stress onto our planet. Automation has helped to ease that stress by applying many optimizations. But now it is time to turn it around and not only slow down but reduce human-made impact on ecosystems. Let us see what could be in the cards.

Next waves in Mechanization

In the First Realm, in Mechanization, a pivotal moment in time was the introduction of James Watt's improved steam engine in 1776. It took until 1908 for the First Industrial Revolution to pick up full speed, and an iconic moment illustrating this momentum was the introduction of Henry Ford's Model T in 1908. His concepts of flow production made full use of the technology available at the time. This period of over 130 years saw numerous improvements in manufacturing technologies. Especially once Electrification and Automation were available to accelerate the Industrial Revolution further. The ability to machine more complex parts with higher precision and at lower cost made innovations like the airplane, space exploration, and the machinery for semiconductor and electronics manufacturing possible. But what comes next in the Realm of Mechanization?

The focus on improving machine tools and manufacturing technologies has been for the last 250 years on processes that take away material from a blank. We also call this subtractive manufacturing. A blank is a standard piece of material like, for example, a length of structural steel. Controlled removal processes such as sawing, drilling, milling, and turning are used to create semi-finished goods that can afterward be combined with methodologies such as welding, soldering, gluing, riveting, pressing and others. The blank is often additionally prepared beforehand by stamping it into a shape, bending, flanging, punching, or forging. Most of these methodologies go back to the early machine tools but the performance has improved enormously over time. Newer technologies for material subtraction include EDM (Electric Discharge Manufacturing), or laser cutting. EDM uses frequent, high voltage discharge to remove material, especially from hard metals. Such metals are used for making drills and other machining bits and are much harder than standard steel. Therefore they can't be machined by conventional tools. Several applications for EDM were developed between the 1940s and 1960s. The 1970s saw the breakthrough of laser cutting for metals, but also textiles and other non-metallic materials.

The alternative to subtractive manufacturing is called additive manufacturing. The first innovation in this space was pottery, and it explains very well the basic idea. Raw material, in the case of pottery clay, is shaped into the intended final form and then cured to obtain the required properties. There is practically no waste. The earliest pottery is known from China and stems from 20'000 BCE. Around 17'000 years later, at the end of the late stone-age, people in India and China learned how to form metal parts into a shape, which, of course, cannot be done by hand. The material - in the beginning, copper - needs to be heated up to its melting point. That could be achieved as early as 5'000 BCE. Copper was not hard enough for effective cutting tools or weapons and was often used for jewelry production. It most likely held high social status, since copper artifacts have frequently been found in graves of persons of high social standing. The invention of bronze, an alloy from copper with an addition of tin, made it possible to make more durable and sturdy tools. But to put it into a useful shape, the traditional ways of forming, like forging, were not effective enough.

Around 3'000 BCE at the highpoint of the Copper Age, the process of casting was introduced. Casting means that a mold is made, and the molten metal or alloy is poured from a crucible into that mold. After cooling off, the mold is removed and the cast part is available. Typically, the cast parts need to be further machined with subtractive methods. Over the millennia, the ability to create higher temperatures allowed the melting of substances with higher melting points. The medieval times saw pig iron casting becoming possible.

In the very early stages of Electrification, as we already saw before, galvanoplasty allowed the forming of any shape by layering metal ions onto a model inside an electrolytic bath. But the economic importance was never critical, partially because the process is quite slow. The method of pottery is, in principle, a subset of a broader technology called sintering. Wet clay can be used, as well as dry ceramic powders, to permanently connect by heat treatment. We call the results ceramics or porcelain. Around 1'200 BCE, this method was utilized for metallic material as well. This process did not win the race against casting, though. Much later, sintering did regain practical use in powder metallurgical processes using metal mixtures that are difficult to alloy by smelting.

Additive manufacturing, however, did not receive much groundbreaking innovation thrust for hundreds of years, even though the waste reduction is such an advantage. During the next decades, this will dramatically change with the introduction of 3D printing. Since the first lab tests in 1974, the speed, precision, and available materials for 3D printing are steadily growing. Ten years after the first lab model, the first patents for stereolithography were filed, and in 1986, 3D

Systems, the first company focused entirely on 3D printing, was founded based on such patents. This technology, often referred to as SLA, uses UV light to project a layer of a model into a container filled with monomeric resin, where the UV light causes polymerization. Then the next layer gets projected, and so forth. That allows the creation of very intricate shapes with a smooth surface finish. The disadvantage is that this technology only works for polymer plastics, and multiple colors are not an option. But for certain purposes, it is an ideal technology. Quickly other companies started with different approaches. The most common for lower-end to middle-end applications – in terms of complexity, finish, and mechanical properties – are FDM printers. FDM stands for fused deposition modeling. A plastic filament is fed to a heated extruder, which moves within a build room and deposits molten plastic, layer by layer. It takes quite some time, especially if the model is complex, and there are limitations in terms of which shapes can be modeled. But the methodology is low cost, and there are hundreds of filament types available in different colors that glow at night, with wood or metal mixed in, and various kinds of base plastics. This choice is excellent for prototyping, as well as design objects, or spare parts. One of the most frequently used filament base materials is PLA or polylactic acid. This organic polyester derives entirely from renewable, plant-based sources.

Additionally, it is compostable. It can even be used for medical implants, like plates, screws, or meshes, since it slowly dissolves into lactic acid, which the body can easily absorb. The game-changer has been much more costly metal printers. The Fraunhofer Institut first introduced metal powder bed fusing, utilizing laser beams, in 1995. It allows growing metal parts out of a powder bed, from metals, such as aluminum, steel, copper, titanium, and others, with practically unlimited geometries, hidden channels and voids, and thin walls. Not only does this process save waste, but it does not need molds, which in most casting processes are not reusable. It also allows creating structures with details that are impossible to produce by any other means. The function of parts can be optimized to a degree so far out of reach for engineers. In addition, the operation of this equipment needs far less expertise. One machine handles what a whole workshop of equipment could do before, and more. That allows sending the CAD file of a complicated part to a faraway place and start producing the part right away, saving the shipping of the part. That also extends to the spare parts production, where the time delay of shipping a component can be problematic.

Next waves in Mechanization

I believe that 3D printing and the renaissance of additive manufacturing will be the biggest game changer for Mechanization in the history of humankind. It might well start a new, second Industrialization with impacts similar to those of the second Agricultural Revolution. This time it could help to bring industrial and manufacturing activities to those places on our planet that so far have been excluded from it.

Miniaturization has been a critical driver for the Automation sector, allowing the manufacture of smaller and more powerful semiconductors, and packing more computational performance into chips, which consume less energy. Production of semiconductor devices in the nanometer-scale began in 2013 with the first batches of 16nm devices. The year 2018 saw the first 5nm production. A nanometer (nm) measures one-billionth of a meter or as much as your fingernail grows in one second. It is not only computational power, but also memory chips and components for sensors, which become smaller, cheaper, and more frugal. Now imagine we could also create mechanical structures that are microscopic. On a single waver, we could grow thousands of tiny electric motors, turbines, or pumps. That would allow building machines or vehicles small enough to be injected into the bloodstream of a human being. We could build drones that are so small and lightweight that they would consume almost no energy. The energy supply for a mobile phone could perhaps consist of a microturbine, running on biogas from a cylinder the size of one AAA battery, keeping the phone running for a month. Why would the efficiency be so incredible? The smaller mechanical objects become, the larger is their relative sturdiness. Which, in turn, means that they can be designed a lot lighter and thinner than on the macro-scale.

Take a ceramic vase of average size that holds a lovely bouquet of roses. If you drop the vase from 10cm onto a hard floor, it might not break. Drop it from 30cm and it will inevitably break unless it is made from exceptional ceramics. But let us imagine that from the same ordinary ceramics material, we would make a vase that is only 3mm in circumference. Drop that from 30cm, no problem. No problem at 30m either.

The properties of miniature versions of regular life objects are astonishing. Today, besides nanoscale electronics, critical applications are nanoscale passive materials. For example, nanosized silver particles woven into socks to counter foot odor. Or nanoplastic particles used in toothpaste or cleaning fluids create microabrasion. Sunscreen contains nanoparticles of zinc oxide and deodorants tiny aluminum particles to block sweat glands. This reminds us of the enthusiastic, thoughtless use of many technologies during the early stages of new discoveries. These nanoparticles, once released into the environment, are very difficult to prevent from entering the food chain. Too small for wastewater filtering, these particles travel down rivers into lakes and oceans, where they are absorbed by life forms. Technological impact assessments are urgently needed for these kinds of convenience applications.

Hopefully the focus will soon shift towards nanomachinery, which could complement the efforts in 3D printing. The creation of nanoelectronics with nanoscopic 3D printing could be a step change.

Huge steps in Energization

What about the Realm of Energization then? Our ability to utilize primary energy sources, whether directly or for electricity generation, has tempted humanity into overuse. The CO_2 baggage of the Second Industrial Revolution haunts us – and all life – on planet earth, in the form of human-induced climate change. While nature does not mind and will adapt, many species, including humankind, will suffer. All focus of the next wave of innovation in the field of Energization needs to be on CO_2 neutrality of the energy that fuels our economic system. The aspect that is well underway and will not slow down no matter what is the exploitation of renewable energy. It is economically so viable to use sun, wind, geothermal energy, and hydropower, that broad penetration of the potential is just a matter of time. The overall demand structure of energy will need two things, though: much more - if not limitless - electric power, and supply stability. That stability needs to come from the right mix of decentralized generation, larger utility generation plants, and energy storage systems. The latter is necessary to align differences in supply and demand of energy in light of volatile, renewable power. The conventional concept of base load capacities does not apply to the degree often claimed. The more intermeshed national or regional power pools are, the more the misalignments between supply and demand of renewable sources are evened out. A major source of stabilization can come from dispatchable renewables, such as hydro dams, the heat storage of CSP systems (concentrated solar power), or gas tanks, containing biogas or gas produced from surplus renewables during low demand times. Battery storage will play a role as well, though likely not only as a dedicated storage system but also as a by-product of battery-based electric vehicles. Technologies to further drive energy efficiency are often the most profitable way to tackle energy demand.

Already today, we see a decoupling of economic growth from the growth of power consumption, mainly due to progress in energy efficiency. We have to thank the Third Realm for that, Automation. In this future scenario, we will not find too many plants that are slow in adapting their generation output, as it used to be with large-scale coal and nuclear plants. The concept of base load was conceived for these types of rigid plants, to give them a spot in the overall system. In this new scenario, we will have most of the load covered by intermittent, renewable sources, which partially compensate each other's volatility, while the rest of stability is ensured by fast-acting gas and hydropower plants. The key is the ability to have energy reserves at any time and a mix that can provide the right reserves to each application. Hydro dams can act as giant "water batteries," power to gas can be used to provide gas reserves, and electric mobility with its millions of batteries is another source of reserves. Power to gas means that surplus renewable power, for example, during sunny, windy days, with high run-of-the-river hydro generation is used to crack water into hydrogen and oxygen. This hydrogen gas can be stored, or reformed into hydrocarbon fuel gases, by removing CO_2 from the atmosphere. The gases can be used for fuel cells onboard vehicles, for gas turbines, or to derive liquid fuels, for example, for airplanes.

What about the issue mentioned above of "much more, if not limitless energy?" While a sound balance of storage, network interconnectivity, and renewables mix will likely be able to supply us with enough energy to run our economies, several activities will need enormous amounts of power. The top three of these have to do with water, agriculture, and space.

The last decades have seen the number of military conflicts, civilian and combat troop casualties, and victims from terror declining to the lowest level for hundreds of years. While that might feel different when watching the news, the facts show a clear picture. We still have a way to go to reduce this further and to ensure sustainable peace. The primary antagonist of peace is injustice. When people feel that they do not have sufficient access to the resources they need for their livelihood - like food, water, medicine, and education - they become first frustrated, then aggressive, and finally desperate. That is the point where war, civil war, belligerent civil unrest, and terrorism spawn. Eradicating the injustice that leads to all of this is the best way to ensure or restore peace.

Over the last around 100 years, most conflicts on our planet were about energy sources. That is the reason why so many armed conflicts, as well as terror movements, are in – or stem from – countries that actually possess energy resources. That is either because an aggressor uses military power to obtain oil or gas from such countries, or it is because the local population feels they are being robbed and resorts to unrest or even terror. The new energy scenario described above should slowly but surely curb this, especially if network interconnectivity creates an interdependent partnership between the nations of our world. The next conflicts will, unfortunately, be about a resource that has a far more immediate impact on people's lives: water. During the course of thousands of years, and even today, there have been numerous conflicts about water and water rights. But with growing populations, especially in arid regions with climate change-induced droughts, and due to the water-intensive lifestyle of those who can afford, water scarceness will become a serious problem. It will be the number one source of perceived injustice. If humankind were able to provide enough water, this would not only save people from dying of thirst, but also help prevent many armed conflicts.

Seawater desalination is the key, large-scale technology to achieve that. Smaller-scale systems, like heat exchangers or fog traps, which both harvest water from the atmosphere's humidity, will play a role in smaller, remote communities. But to supply large urban areas and the agricultural sector, megascale water plants are necessary. There are different processes to desalinate water, and much progress has been made.

Nevertheless, large amounts of energy are needed to reach the point where natural water tables, rivers, and lakes are no longer suffering from our civilization's thirst. And obviously, the water needs to be produced CO_2 neutrally. Otherwise, we amplify climate change, a key reason for desertification and water scarcity.

The second cause of injustice is the lack of nutrition. Like the lack of clean water, it has a direct impact on health, life expectancy, and productivity of people. It therefore drives a sense of injustice well beyond just the economic impact of high food prices. To feed the world, we must not rely on conventional farming. It takes too much space. Because of that, rainforests are destroyed to make room for soybean farming or palm oil plantations. Nature is pushed back, habitats are destroyed for cattle herding or to win more arable land. Ironically, most of this newly created arable land

200

is then used in the most ineffective ways, with mediocre yield rates and substandard soil protection. At the peak of the human population on earth in around 100 years from now, with slightly above eleven billion, we need to be able to feed every single human, but not at the cost of destroying our planet. We need to reduce not only our CO_2 footprint but also our geographical footprint. For that, highly compact agriculture is needed. That would make use of vertical farms, hydroponics, aquaponics, 24-hour lighting, hothouses, and soil conserving technologies. Even meat products will be produced in vitro, at least for end uses that are anyhow highly processed, like pizza toppings, ground meat, or wok dishes. All this needs energy.

The final energy hog has less to do with injustice, but rather with a mix of precaution, science, and curiosity: space travel. There are good reasons to speak up for or against space travel. Orbital activities are not the issue; to put satellites into space, we will always be able to come up with the fuel. However, if we talk about manned space exploration within our solar system, or even beyond, we talk about giant amounts of energy. Regardless of whether this energy is provided in chemical form, electromagnetic form, or yet another way, we first would need to have vast amounts of CO_2 neutral secondary energy available.

These three vectors of energy demand, which go far beyond the business-as-usual case, will need cheap, CO_2 neutral, and democratized energy. That means power available for all countries at an affordable cost, and in amounts that prevent energy from being an insurmountable hurdle to implement these grant schemes. Nuclear fission - the process used in today's nuclear power plants - is often mentioned as the solution for this. New fission reactors are supposed to be less risky, using more abundant fuel minerals, producing less radioactive waste, and avoiding weapons-grade byproducts. But it does not change the fact that there would be radioactive waste and that the mining process means large-scale encroachment upon nature. The better alternative seems to be fusion reactors. Those mimic the process happening on our sun, the original source of all our renewable energy. The fundamental process combines two parts of hydrogen, which join to make one part of helium. Only a tiny fraction of the hydrogen we already produce today would be needed to power all energy needs of humanity. The resulting end product is helium, which is inert and occurs naturally in our atmosphere, and depending on the utilized technology, inevitable low-risk byproducts can build up. The fusion process itself has been proved feasible on earth. Since pressures like in the center of the sun are not possible, the fusion process needs higher temperatures than on the sun. To create these is possible. What is difficult is to contain the resulting super-hot plasma without consuming more energy than is being produced by the reactor. For quite some time, the effort was very much bundled into one massive multi-government project: ITER, or International Thermonuclear Reactor. But when only one horse is on the race circuit, the speed is perhaps not the highest. Once a race starts, humans are incredibly motivated and ingenious. That is happening now, with over a dozen start-up companies working on smaller projects, each deploying slightly different variants of the base technologies used. While ITER has been painstakingly slow to achieve progress, the start-ups go for far smaller designs and multiply the number of bets. In the meantime, ITER is often criticized for its 25 BUSD total budget. But compared to the annual 500 BUSD of subsidies going into hydrocarbon fuels, this bet is rather small. We are confident that ITER and the many start-ups create a race that will have the first commercial fusion reactor within ten years.

Such fusion reactors will need ten million times less fuel than a conventional thermal power plant. And the fuel is the most abundant material on earth - hydrogen. For the Realm of Energization, this could be the most significant game changer ever.

Automation in the 21st century

When Automation started in Neolithic times with traps, the core idea was that the trap would act like an automated hunter and perform its task without any human intervention or even presence. That was the whole purpose of these first automatons, to allow their human owners to rest, sleep, or be busy with other tasks while the trap does its work. When Automation regained importance as a tool for Industrialization, the aim was more to allow one human to control more machinery or a team to supervise more production assets. Take a miller in a 19th-century grain mill. Before, he had to continually monitor the production, check the filling level of various vessels, and then intervene accordingly. The introduction of Automation allowed the miller to trust in automated processes and walk up and down a long aisle of mill stands, adjust speeds, check the condition of equipment, or fill in report cards. Only once the automatic process stopped and demanded attention, the operator had to focus on that particular mill stand for intervention.

The same applies in principle with large process automation systems. A decision made by an operator, for example, to fill a blender with a set of ingredients and to start the initial blending process, triggers a whole range of actions, as defined in the batch recipe. The sequence of adding feedstock elements and the values - the amounts, which temperature the blender vat has to be brought to, which speed the blender has to run for, and for how long - are defined and automatically executed. Once the program reaches a set point, the operator gets this information and decides to release the compound towards the next production step. As we saw before, the more modern and powerful the control system of that plant is the more input and output signals, assets, and process steps a single operator can handle. The control system not only drives up labor productivity but also helps to avoid human error. Take the dosage part of the above process. If a human would have to add several dozen substances, with different speeds and amounts, it would only be a matter of time before there is a slip in a line in the recipe or a misread of a quantitative specification. The system does not make such mistakes, and at every step runs cross-checks within fractions of a second. Nevertheless, there is still always a human in the loop. Every major production step needs the authorization of the operator. Sometimes, for critical process steps, even the synchronized approval by a second operator, or the shift manager, is needed.

In our households, we would be quite frustrated if the washing machine would prompt us every couple of minutes before dispensing the detergent, or once the appliance has determined it is time to tumble the laundry. We expect the entire process to run through, from start to end. When we press the start button on our robot vacuum cleaner, we want to be able to go away and let the little machine do its job, while we might go for a walk. Well, it is fascinating to watch the robot, at least the first couple of times. This way of thinking will inevitably enter other domains as well. As human beings, we are rightfully cautious when it comes to autonomous systems. As a first step, we continuously monitor all activity. After a while, we resort to some checkpoints where we still insist on authorizing. And eventually we let the system run autonomously, but we stick around for exceptional cases. To fully trust an autonomous system - to not have any human in the loop and to not be on stand-by - takes a leap of faith. In the case of the vacuum robot, we dare to do this already, since the perceived risks are low enough. For a petrochemical complex, we might remain anxious for quite some time.

On the Energization front, we will see a trend towards 100% renewable energy. That will allow us to lift taxes on hydrocarbon use and resulting emissions dramatically, and effectively end the era of internal combustion engines. As a result, road-based mobility will become 100% electric. Vehicles will become significantly simpler, with only a fraction of the parts, will be less suitable as a status symbol, and will most likely be less and less owned by individual owners, but instead shared on demand. That means that large vehicle fleets will be owned by for-profit companies that need to maximize return on capital employed. For that, vehicles need to be in productive use for most of the time. Today, privately owned cars are used for an average of 300 hours per year or around 3.5% of the time. They are among the least leveraged assets on our planet. The only way to drive fleet usage to utilization levels competing with best-in-class industrial asset utilization is to automate the entire operation of such fleets. Dispatch systems will use software tools to match which vehicle serves which client. Heuristic algorithms will optimize when, where, and which car is to be recharged or refueled with hydrogen. The routing will, of course, be automated, using navigation systems. Predictive maintenance systems will utilize hosts of sensor data to predict when a car has to be taken off the road for service.

But most importantly, the cars will not carry a driver. The primary reason for that is not so much cost, though there is a savings effect, of course. The primary goal is practicality. A driver can only be active for a certain amount of time, perhaps eight hours. The twelve-hour taxi shifts we see in some countries are not only too tough on the drivers but also generate safety risks. Drivers need to meet with another driver to hand over the vehicle, which creates revenue drops twice a day.

Additionally, the car has one less space for passengers. To think that operators in control rooms could remotely control several vehicles is not realistic and would bring back safety concerns due to human error. No, the cars need to be in fully autonomous mode. Now, this is a very different risk profile compared to a tumble dryer or a vacuum robot. Now we talk about the risks associated with road traffic, about interactions between many vehicles, some still manually operated. Pedestrians and stray animals come into the equation. We believe that control room personnel and mobile intervention teams will be necessary to jump in when one of hundreds or thousands of autonomous transport pods finds itself in an unforeseen or exceptional situation. But 99% of the time, the pods will do their job on their own. That will take a lot of research, testing, pilot projects, and adaptations in legislation on infrastructure. It will be the critical driver for Automation progress in the 21st century. Due to the importance of individual transport and the size of this market, it will have the attention, funding, and political willingness to make it a success. As the railway tracks of the Industrialization age and the power lines of the Electrification age, autonomous transport will be the enabler of the next big wave in Automation, Autonomy.

Already today, larger, more expensive transport assets, like spacecrafts and airplanes, are equipped with such Autonomy capabilities. A commercial airliner can start, cruise, and land fully autonomously. The crew is the intervention team, mentioned earlier. On an airplane, this team has to be on board - there is no other way. In the case of autonomous trains, this is not needed, and we already find many examples of such driverless trains. Drones for delivery tasks and autonomous marine vessels will follow swiftly.

Will we see fully autonomous industrial plants? Some other trends might help with that: miniaturization and modularization. Two factors used to make an industrial process expensive: the necessary minimum set of personnel to operate it and the costly range of sensors and measurement devices to control it. The latter is changing dramatically. Due to the progress of miniaturized, mass-deployed sensors, the percentage of investment costs for a given plant, say a paint producing plant, for the instrumentation has gone down significantly. With high degrees of automation, centralized control rooms, several plants supervised by a small set of operators, and the possibility to pull in experts with remote control and collaboration systems, the number of personnel needed for a plant has gone down significantly. All this means that smaller plants closer to the customer become cost-effective enough. The benefits of closer customer proximity and less transport distance start to outweigh the scale advantage of large, centralized plants. But the demand covered by such a decentralized plant is smaller. Thus the capacity needs to be a lot lower. Here, modularization enters the stage. Design, engineering, product procurement, installation, testing, and final commissioning for a chemical plant all require substantial effort. Modularization allows us to cut down this effort. Like Lego blocks, pre-engineered, standardized modules are put together, including the respective control logic, and a smaller scale plant can be assembled within a short time. The modules are skid-mounted and can be factory tested before being trucked to the site.

All this cuts down on cost and time. In many areas, we will see such module-based, smaller-scale plants. There will not be a full operations crew on site. Remote operation will allow a dozen such plants to be controlled from one central control room. The risk that such a much smaller plant presents is lower than for a large-scale mother ship. It will be deemed feasible to make such a small plant autonomous, much earlier than that decision would be taken for a giant chemical complex.

Another area where Autonomy will play a significant role is agriculture. The main obstacle - compared to an industrial plant - that farmers face is that their production asset is not homogeneous, engineered, and standardized. Farmland is, fortunately, still a part of nature. But with the trend towards highly compact farming, for example, vertical, hydroponic farming, the process becomes very much engineered and standardized. A vertical farm uses the structural properties of urban environments. In modern urban areas, people live in high-rise buildings. It would be ideal to grow a major part of nutrition for the citizens right around them, inside the city. For that, hydroponic farming units could be stacked on top of each other, covering the walls or structures of buildings. Aquaponic farms, where plants and aquatic animals are cultivated in a cross-fertilizing system, could also be designed for dedicated buildings, and in three dimensions. The output density of such farming concepts is enormous, compared to conventional arable farming or stock farming. Besides, these agricultural concepts allow more Automation than traditional ways, and soon Robotization and eventually even Autonomy.

In the realm of Automation, we will be witnesses of Autonomy, or at least partial Autonomy, in major value streams of our economies, such as transport and logistics, personal transportation, agriculture, industrial processes, and manufacturing. What started with our household appliances will soon be business as usual all around us.

CHAPTER ELEVEN

Digitalization – the Fourth Industrial Revolution

Before diving into the Fourth Industrial Revolution, we should quickly review the properties of the Fourth Realm of Innovation. The reason we call this realm Informatization, as described in more detail in chapter 5, is because its inventions deal with information. What started with proto-language about 100'000 years ago to give us oracy, developed from around 70'000 years ago towards symbols and scripts, adding literacy. Around 40'000 years ago, the symbolization of numbers and swiftly after that, simple arithmetic, gave us numeracy. Then for a long time, Informatization benefited from a host of inventions addressing how information could be stored, multiplied, and transmitted. During that time period, the expression of Informatization that gained the most traction in a scientific sense was mathematics. In turn, mathematics was the most powerful enabler for science and technology across all realms.

The biggest impact on the economy stemmed from the Dawn of Trade, which was made possible by literacy and numeracy as the base for contracting and accounting. Once the age of Robotization gave us computers, this of course accelerated trade, allowed massive processing of data, and powerful heuristics in the area of mathematics. But there is something else that is new. Computers permit us to represent enormous amounts of data in a way that allows us to intuitively understand their meaning. In the simplest form, this could be a two-dimensional sketch of a series of value pairs. But why can we understand such a graph? Let us look back at the origins of this. During the last centuries BCE, mathematicians like Pythagoras or Euclid invented the first graphical representations of mathematical relations. They had to virtually invent a completely new way to illustrate their insights, called geometry. While artists, starting with the first cave paintings, learned how to mimic reality with better and better artistic methods and skills, these paintings, drawings, or sculptures did not express mathematics or data, but rather the appearance of real things and human emotions attached to them. Geometry, literally meant to 'measure the earth', to represent proportions, distances, data. In the 13th century the Arabic world saw the first technical drawings that explained how machines were constructed and operated. That laid the foundation for technical drawing as a core tool for progress in the area of Mechanization. The drawing of a chain pump by al-Jazari from 1205 is an impressive example. The Middle Ages saw the birth of architectural drawings based on planar geometric projection, a technique most likely invented by Filippo Brunelleschi around 1420. In 1718, Leonard Christoph Sturm released his book "Vollständige Mühlenbaukunst" (Comprehensive Art of Mill Construction), which for the first time had a complete set of technical drawings, showing all machines and components drawn in scale.

Geometry, and its principles, is the concept that is used when showing numeric data in a graph. While the ability to understand such graphs is not explicitly taught at school, children already develop the ability to intellectually glean from the illustration what it stands for. We call this skill graphicacy. At school students typically enjoy dedicated classes for languages, writing, and math - for oracy, literacy, and numeracy. But not for graphicacy. It is curious, since graphics are powerful! They are much more concise than a lengthy text that could describe the same. They stick. It is far easier to remember a graph than the long series of numbers it represents. But the most powerful advantage is that graphs make even complex relationships between data items apparent. Humans with sufficient education are able to interpret meaning contained in the data by analyzing the properties of a graph. Both methods - to apply analytical interpretation, like for example creating a trend line, and an intuitive interpretation of, say, a graph showing share prices - are part of this human ability.

Computers make it possible to plot two- or three-dimensional graphs of huge data sets in no time. They also generate animations, which can show a 3D data set over time, adding a fourth dimension. This important development has multiplied the possibilities of graphicacy and has made it one of the most powerful bits of progress in Informatization. It is time to make graphicacy a dedicated part of school education.

The precondition for computer-based graphicacy is of course that data is digitalized. Let us have a look at the beginnings of Digitalization.

The cradle of Digitalization

We find much dissonance in the current discussion on the topic of Digitalization. Some shout that an Industrial Revolution is being proclaimed before it even happens. Others - rightfully so - criticize that too many are joining the bandwagon, calling activities 'Digitalization' that are simply business as usual, typically conventional Automation. This behavior, driven by communications departments in large corporations and spokespersons of ministries, anxious to project an image of progress or to be ahead of the peloton, does nothing but create confusion and devaluation of the concept. The same applies when media discover the topic and present it as a brand new phenomenon. There is a need to clarify and define what Digitalization really is. It has gone on for quite a while, like a wave building up far from shore that is now breaking and unfolding the majority of its energy.

The year that embodies the start of Industrialization was the year 1776 when James Watt presented his vastly improved steam engine. Around a century later, in the notorious year of 1878, Joseph Swan introduced the vacuum light bulb. In a year like no other, so many prominent companies in the Electrification field were founded and important patents in this field were filed. It took only half a century for Robotization to start in 1933 with the unveiling of IBM's Type 285, the first electric computer. Another quarter of a century after that, Digitalization started. In 1954, IMR (Intelligent Machines Research Corporation) won an order from US publishing house Reader's Digest to make use of its technology of digital optical character recognition or short OCR. Typewritten sales reports in their book subscription department were scanned with OCR, creating digital records. In 1957 the National Bureau of Standards created the first-ever digital scan of an image. The five-by-five centimeter, black and white image was scanned with 176 pixels per axis and showed a baby by the name of Walden. Two years later, MIT researcher Douglas T. Ross coined the term CAD, Computer Aided Design. The 1960s witnessed the development of the first 3D CAD systems. The first electrical digital alarm clock was patented in 1957 by D.E Protzmann, while miniaturization allowed the first digital wristwatch by Hamilton Watch Company, the Pulsar, to enter the market in 1970. The clock used an LED display. Two years before, Hamilton had product-placed a prototype of its watch in Stanley Kubrick's groundbreaking science fiction movie "2001: A Space Odyssey". Three years later, the idea to use highly precise digital clocks on satellites to create a digital navigation system was born. In 1980 this so-called GPS, or Global Positioning System, was used for a civil purpose for the first time. In 1990 Japanese carmaker Mazda introduced the first-ever car with a GPS navigation system. Norman Joseph Woodland had the idea for a tagging system for goods, using black and white stripes. He was employed by IBM in 1951, but they did not yet see the time was right for that invention. That changed in 1971 at an industry meeting of the National Association of Food Chains (NAFC), where RCA demonstrated a concept very close to Woodland's 'Bullseye' concentric code system. IBM reacted quickly and reactivated Woodland to develop UPC, the Universal Product Code. This bar code system became the de facto standard for North America, Europe, Australia, and New Zealand. Today, barcoding is broadly used, not only in trade, but also on manufacturing shop floors, in hospitals, government offices, and in logistics operations. It's younger brother, the two-dimensional QR-code, is used to link a user who scans the code on a product or document to a Web page with further content about it. Talking about the Web. Its underlying Informatization technology, the Internet, was an invention of the 1960s as well. It all started with ARPANET. The Advanced Research Projects Agency (ARPA), a part of the US Department of Defense, was eager to develop a communications network for computers that would withstand major disruptions and destruction of entire parts of the network infrastructure. Conventional telecoms networks - all of them analog - could be used to transmit digital data. But if the connection between two computers was cut, the transmission stopped. An ARPA team around Paul Baran developed a packet-switching concept, where bits of digital information could be routed on ever-different paths, through a mesh of nodes. This concept, governed by the Network Control Program, became the Transmission Control Protocol/Internet Protocol, or short TCP/IP, which is the base of today's Internet. The advantage is obvious - if a connection is cut, the transmission commences through alternative nodes. The fact that packets might not arrive in their original sequence does not matter. They are simply arranged in sequence, once all have arrived. Using the

The cradle of Digitalization

Internet was a rather cryptic endeavor and for quite a while a domain only for scientists and tech-nerds. In 1989 British scientist Tim Berners-Lee invented the World Wide Web, or short the Web, an interlinked system where so-called URLs, or Uniform Resource Locators, identified information assets on the Internet. Berners-Lee, working at the European particle accelerator CERN near Geneva, wanted to create a system for CERN researchers and personnel to browse the immense treasure of information and data that CERN provided. The idea was to also mark the information up with meta tags that would allow linking from a place in a document to another document. Since users were running different computer systems to view information, the idea was to have a metalanguage that would ensure that such meta tagged documents would display in the same way, independent of platform. He called the idea to augment text with such additional linkage and formatting information hypertext. Together with his Belgian friend Robert Cailliau, he proposed the system, including HTML, the coding language, on November 12, 1990. They called their Hypertext project WWW for World Wide Web. Still today, URLs start with www. A NeXT computer served as the first web server in history. During December of that year, Berners-Lee completed all tools and components for a functioning Web.

On December 20, 1990, he published the first-ever Web page, which described the project itself. I believe that the Web is the single most powerful innovation vector of the Fourth Industrial Revolution. Like a magnet, it attracted countless additional inventions.

Maybe this is the moment to compare a principle difference between the other Realms of Innovation and their specific Industrial Revolutions to Informatization and Digitalization. When innovation happens, for example, in the Realm of Automation, it starts with a problem that needs a solution. Let us say a miller is annoyed by the fact that he has a huge head box containing grain, but the flour sack is much smaller. When the sack is full, and the mill does not stop grinding, there will be a mess. It would be practical to have an automatic mechanism to disengage the millstones from the windmill vanes when the sack is full, by pulling the transmission gear. That problem is presented to engineers who come up with a whole range of potential fixes. Like a funnel, these ideas are tested, affirmed, or discarded.

Verified ideas are spread into variants and further funneled to a small set of final proposals. One of those survives and is built. That principle also applies to Mechanization and Energization. But in the Realm of Informatization, it has always been somewhat different. Take cave paintings. They did not represent a solution to a predefined problem. They just happened, and our ancestors had no idea what they might be useful for. The applications of stepstone inventions in Informatization typically open an inverted funnel. It starts with a straightforward discovery or idea without a specification, which, over time, blooms into a wide funnel of applications. For corporate management or investors, this is quite unsettling. It goes against the grain to fund a project that has no specified delivery and that yields a result without a clear purpose, even if it has nebulous, awesome potential.

And this applies very much for Digitalization projects in industrial businesses. We will talk about this more in the next chapters.

Preconditions

There are several factors and preconditions for broad industrial Digitalization to happen. Obviously, computers are fundamental to process digital data as is the Internet as a transmission system. For industrial applications, data needs to be acquired from the process. For that, production records as well as condition information about the process and the production assets need to be collected. In the chapters about Robotization, we already discussed control systems for industrial operations. These DCS or PLC systems possess I/O channels to receive or send signals. In a pure play automation concept, system engineers would only have the essential instrumentation devices installed to collect exactly those signals needed to run the operation. The reason for that is that installing and wiring such instruments is cumbersome and the measurement devices are expensive. But there are two effects of the electronics boom in the consumer market - especially the smartphone market - that have changed this. Technology for wireless networking has become dramatically cheaper and miniaturized enough to build wireless capabilities into field instruments. And sensor technology has been made a mass-produced commodity, allowing ubiquitous sensors all around factories and plants. Wireless is also a critical enabler for driving Digitalization beyond fixed assets, covering also mobile assets, which cannot be connected with wires.

Sensors that used to be a rather delicate and complicated set of electronic boards have been merged into system-on-chip assemblies, which are incredibly rugged, tiny, and produced with highly cost-efficient semiconductor methods. Take a GPS assembly. The first GPS receivers for military purposes were the size of a shoebox and cost as much as a car. Today, a GPS can be built into a wristwatch and costs less than five dollars. That is in part made possible by the vastly increased sensitivity of the chip assemblies. Between 1990 and 1998 the sensitivity grew by a factor of 30, and during the next decade by another factor of ten. Today such a commercial system is around one thousand times more sensitive than the first versions were, driving the cost for the complicated antenna down. Host-based GPS reduced the complexity of the chip itself by utilizing the CPU of the host system, for example, the phone.

GPS is one of the most advanced sensors compared to simple physical sensors measuring properties like temperature or humidity. And still, it has become so cheap and tiny that it can be built into any industrial asset, even if in the beginning there is no clearly defined use case yet. Consumer electronics have sifted through each and every sensor type, seeing how these could be used for consumer electronics or appliances. Position sensors and attitude sensors work in handheld game controllers. Shock sensors serve in electronic toys. And, not to forget, still and video cameras have become so ubiquitous that their cost came down so much that they can be installed in hundreds of places in a contemporary production site. This proliferation of affordable sensors creates an avalanche of data, which is the raw material of Digitalization.

How can such an enormous mountain of data, referred to as 'Big Data', be best utilized in businesses? If every device is made capable of storing and processing Big Data, the devices will explode in cost. Besides, the methods and algorithms to make use of the data are developing relentlessly and fast. Each piece of equipment would need to be patched and updated continually, which would be a difficult task to deploy. The performance of field devices would, after a while, inevitably not be sufficient to cope with higher computational demands. The solution for this is to transmit all data to data centers, store it once, redundantly, and have robust, scalable servers to handle the data processing and demanding computations. Such servers are like potent computers, optimized for massive data crunching. Instead of updating thousands of field devices, software updates only happen in the data center. If the computational needs grow, the data center adds some more servers. The central, redundant storage also prevents data losses. This concept is called a 'cloud service.' Data is sent to the cloud, which is a synonym for the central storage and computing of Big Data. For especially confidential trade data, the same principles apply and can be implemented within the control sphere of a business, as a so-called private cloud.

Let us look at a typical example, which says a lot about how Digitalization works. In the late 1990s, a friend joined a company that employed motorcycle drivers who carried backpacks with a laptop, a GPS, and some additional electronics. They systematically drove down every single road in Germany, capturing where it started, ended, what name it carried, and what the speed limit was. The company worked on a nationwide, so-called, metalayer of information for navigation maps. The underlying maps themselves were digitally scanned conventional road maps.

At the same time, Intrinsic Graphics, a video game company in the US, had created a rendering kernel that was able, in real time, to project satellite imagery onto a virtual globe and spin that globe while zooming in and out. What was meant as a software library for game developers quickly caught attention, and Keyhole Inc. was spun out to develop the technology further. Especially the real-time streaming of massive satellite images to users, and the technique to overlay several image sources and other mark-up information, made the Keyhole product very powerful. In

2004 Google acquired Keyhole. The intention was to serve customers of their search engine better. To allow additional use cases, the layering methodology could be used to display specific information layers. Soon after, Google started adding street-level images for its groundbreaking Street View addition. The amount of data users accessed when starting up Google Maps or Google Earth reached around twenty-one petabytes, or twenty-one million gigabytes in 2012, and has been growing ever since. No one could have stored that amount of information on a mobile device or laptop. No one would want the daily update packages to hit their email inbox. It has to reside in the cloud. And no one would have imagined the many uses for this cloud-based service at the time that Google executives took the bold decision to enhance this service. Very typically for Digitalization innovations, the funnel of applications only opened up after the introduction of the technology, only after enormous upfront investment and effort.

In summary, besides computers and the Internet, the preconditions for the Digitalization of industries are ubiquitous sensors, cloud services, and wireless technologies.

Current developments and challenges

Processes outside of the industrial core activities have been digitalized since computers were introduced in areas such as accounting, payroll, or financial services. Industrial companies, therefore, had experience in operating computer systems, corporate networks, or even entire in-house data centers. For supply chain optimization and sales & marketing, web interfaces became a standard tool. Transaction data, like purchase orders, invoices, or Kanban messages, were exchanged in the form of XML telegrams. But in the early 2000s, the factory or plant operation was still isolated from this thinking. Information Technology, or IT, was restricted to the non-operations part of a company. While in all other activities, industry-standard IT allowed seamless integration, the running of software from different vendors on one system, plug & play of office hardware, and compatibility within and between companies, it looked very different on the shop floor.

Machine automation and plant control systems employed industry-standard communication protocols. Otherwise, field instruments or actuators, such as conveyors or valves, could not have been addressed. But every vendor had a different way to furnish information about its products, which made it impossible to have an integrated view of all production assets. Only the core signaling between controllers, field devices, and actuators was digitalized. Everything else was either paper-based or even invisible. While in an office environment employees were able to use a graphical user interface such as Microsoft Windows with its apps to browse all kind of information, copy & paste a paragraph of text from a brochure to reuse in a presentation file, then connect a printer with plug & play, and finally print this new document, all these advances had not touched the production side of things. ERP systems (Enterprise Resource Planning) allowed seamless integration of all transactional systems in a company, from bank accounts to invoicing, treasury to financial planning, from payroll to keeping track of work hours. Such a powerful integration system with an intuitive user interface did not exist for production operations.

In the early years of the new millennium, a team of Automation researchers and engineers in ABB's Swedish outfit in rural Västerås started thinking about what the next step in industrial Automation could be. ABB had been a pioneer in DCS or Distributed Control Systems, and by organic and acquisitive activity had maneuvered itself into the globally leading spot in this field. But what could be the next big thing in the world of DCS? Inspired by the ease of use, compatibility, and market penetration of Microsoft's product suite, the team aspired to build something that would do for a customer on the operations side what IT was doing for the administration side. They coined the term Industrial IT or IIT for this. The idea was to marry Information Technology and Operational Technology, IT and OT, in one system.

On the back of the DCS as a connectivity vehicle to all plant assets, IIT should connect to all information assets relevant for the production process. That would allow filling a data container, or data object, with all these different aspects of a real-world physical asset. This data item they named an Aspect Object. A plant operator in the control room could now click on a physical asset, for example, a mixer, and not only control the mixer by switching it on and off, but could get operations data, like rounds per minute. With a right-button mouse click, the operator could now open the Aspect Object view of this machine and see all the information aspects of it. These could be documents about the device, like the original purchase order, invoice, warranty documents, spare part lists, drawings, or a photograph. The aspects could also be data, such as maintenance history, the exact geospatial position, a live feed from a supervision camera, or a recommended tool set for a service intervention. The connection with the ERP system allowed the operator to see if spare parts were readily available on the shelf, and, if not, if they could be ordered and from which supplier or distributor. Another integration layer was with maintenance management systems. Computerized maintenance management or CMMS was until then a separate system, somewhere between IT and OT. With those systems being built into the IIT system, or being integrated with it, operators could analyze a potential need for a service intervention, check the needed tools and parts, find out about available service personnel, and by tapping into the ERP's production planning data, to figure out the best moment to effect such a maintenance action. Once that was defined, the IIT system would create a service ticket, which popped up on the handheld CMMS device of the respective service engineer, who also received access to the correct Aspect Object with all its data. After closing the service intervention, this information could now be routed back to the control system, and the maintenance record updated. With this breakthrough in the conceptual expansion of what plant control could be, ABB was at least a decade ahead of all competition. Since the framework went far beyond conventional Automation, the term Extended Automation System was introduced, and the ABB System 800 control system added 'XA' to its name. Today, System 800XA is the market-leading DCS worldwide and still conceptually ahead of other systems. Eventually, Industrial^{IT}©, a term copyright-protected by ABB, would be called the Internet of Things, or IoT, and the Aspect Objects are nowadays referred to as Digital Twin.

In the early 2000s, operators were trained with so-called online process simulators. That allowed taking a scenario from a real plant condition situation and to have the operator try out how to react and run the plant. Without creating any damage, danger, or waste, the operator could learn and improve. Today's plants are covered in sensors, running back vast amounts of data to the control system, which is stored in so-called librarian systems. These act as a data-warehouse, holding status data of every aspect of the plant, every move of an operator's computer mouse, and even contextual data, such as weather data or market price trends. This Big Data is the fodder for advanced data analytics. Instead of a human operator training a situation in real time, the control system can run through thousands of scenarios a million times faster, learning how to optimize the outcome of regular operations and to mitigate crises. Over time, this will allow plants to become more and more autonomous. Already today, it will enable us to drive plant performance beyond the point of human capabilities - soon parts of plants will work entirely on their own. Even quite complex parts of process plants become - from a plant designer's view - just a black box building block. The plant design will include the assembly of such plant building blocks physically, while dragging and dropping the control system representations and control logic on a screen into place, automatically making the building blocks function and interact with each other. That will allow us to design plants faster, make them smaller scale, run them remotely, and with little personnel. It will also allow us to take apart, mobilize, and redeploy these building blocks to form new production lines, following the changes of markets and demand.

An area where modern Robotization and Digitalization can work hand in hand to change the nature of business forever is in mining. A conventional mining operation consists of several stages, with heavy machinery at their center. Let us take the example of an underground mine for gold. Once a deposit has been proven, one or several main shafts and a service shaft have to be sunk. Mine hoists will be constructed in the bigger main shafts, and an auxiliary system for personnel and emergencies in the smaller one. A mine hoist is, in principle, an elevator. A typical elevator in a high-rise building - except for some record-breaking specimens - can reach several hundred meters, carry about a one ton of load, and travel with around ten meters per second. Mine hoists are made to transport a lot more cargo, faster and further. The deepest single-lift hoist for mining at Moab Khotsong gold mine in South Africa's North West bridges 3'150 meters, runs at twenty meters per second, and carries twenty-three tons. Even hoists with more than sixty tons are in operation, harnessing ten megawatts of electric power.

The hoists bring miners and equipment to the rock face underground and bring ore back up to the surface. The deeper the mining level, the more the temperatures rise. That, together with frequent high humidity, limited oxygenation, and buildup of dust, makes it essential to ventilate the mine. These ventilation systems can easily have two times five MW motors, as much as 150 average cars at maximum power output. Similarly, in many deep mines, water is an issue and massive pumps are employed to keep the water from drowning the active part of the site. Additional equipment, such as personnel carriages, conveyor belt systems, wheel loaders, and jumbo drills, are in operation. On the top side, the payload coming off the hoists needs to be processed. Large grinders and crushers take down the size of the ore as it comes off the mine. Sizing and concentration processes are used to create a higher density of the wanted mineral. All these steps used to be individually operated and controlled. Between all stages of handling material, buffers were built up to ensure that the process can continue, even if particular equipment has to be taken offline or is slowing down. People had to be present in all parts of the mining process and close to the equipment. For a comparable activity, different mining companies or operations needed a similar amount of power, people, and capital. Profitability depended mostly on the yield rate, as a function of the ore grade of the respective deposit. The more grams of gold were in a ton of rock, the more profitable the mine was. But Digitalization has changed that. Modern mining companies equip all their machines, both fixed and mobile, with sensors and wireless communication interfaces. Equipment, such as wheel loaders or mining trucks, can then be remotely controlled.

The same applies to all equipment that can be connected to a DCS. That allows having significantly fewer personnel at the rock face, which not only eliminates long travel times to get there but also reduces risks for miners. With people only being present in some areas of the mine, the ventilation can be adjusted to work perfectly just in those areas. We call this ventilation-on-demand. Instead of running the fans on full speed, all the time, consuming megawatt-hours of electricity, the ventilation is adaptively tailored to the actual need, at all times. From the location of breaking out rock material, through all handling processes, conveying, and hoisting, no human needs to touch the ore. Sensors scan the material flow at every stage, predicting the optimal flow and even analyzing the likely composition of the material. Material arriving on the surface is automatically stored in long rows by large machines called a stacker. The Digitalization system completely controls those. While the stacker forms the stockpile, the system keeps a virtual inventory of the ore grade content of the pile. That allows the other machine working with it, the so-called reclaimer, to retrieve the optimal mix of material to feed the next processing step, the crusher. All these optimized processes save twenty to thirty percent of the energy usually consumed. The human productivity goes up, while at the same time taking humans out of harm's way. The better control over the material properties and stockpiling keeps inventories lower and make the entire process smoother. Since the complete mining site is covered with sensors, the control room does not need to be right next to the action. It can be in a less remote place, for example in an office block in a city. That again removes the need to transport numbers of people to far away isolated places. In the future of mining, the majority of the personnel will no longer be exposed to harsh conditions, long non-productive travel, and extended periods away from their families. Instead, they will sit in front of control screens, supervising robotized machines and vehicles, and after the shift is over, they will return to their families. At the same time, mines with lower ore grades have a chance to be operated with such improved productivity that they can be as profitable as a 'lucky strike' mine. Take, for example, Boliden's Garpenberg mine, North of Stockholm, in Sweden.

Since 2014, Garpenberg has been dubbed the most integrated mine in the world, using every then available means of Digitalization and Robotization. All skips, conveyors, and hoists are fully automated. Underground process equipment, electric utility systems, ventilation, pumping, and minerals processing are seamlessly integrated. That allowed the mine to lift its output by 60% while cutting operational costs significantly. The zinc, silver, and lead mine, which started operations in the 13th century, has far lower ore quality than numerous competitive mines, but has - through its Internet of Things approach - developed into Boliden's most profitable mining site. Only a fraction of the personnel is near the rock face, and overall the personnel are distributed over thirty-three workplaces. Remote experts can be looped in from afar to help in case a tricky problem occurs. The operation has more than 400 motors, almost 300 power electronic drives, and thousands of sensors, all working in one integrated system.

But what if a complex operation is not only demanding in terms of control and optimization, but is actually even moving around? Liquefied natural gas, or LNG, allows for transportation of this valuable raw material across the globe on giant vessels, on LNG tankers. Such a ship is not just a carrier that is loaded up by cranes and has only the function to propel the vessel and its freight from A to B; an LNG tanker is in principle a floating chemical plant. Liquefaction of the gas happens onshore in a gas processing facility, but the entire process of preparing the tanks, loading the gas, keeping the conditions right, cooling, pumping, and of course the propulsion, navigation, and docking has to be conducted by the vessel before the discharging of the cargo can be done. LNG needs to be kept at very low temperatures of around negative 163 degrees centigrade, which is the point at which the gas changes to a liquid state on sea level altitude. During the entire transport cycle, the gas must continue to be cooled like this, by cry-technology. Loading liquid gas into the tanks is a delicate process. The gas is so cold it would damage the tanks and pumps. The tanks need to be prepared, to have low oxygen levels to avoid combustion. There are several steps to gas up, and then cool down the tanks. All operations of moving the LNG are conducted by the vessel's pump systems. The tankers typically have four or five separate tanks, each with three pumps. During the transport, a part of the LNG re-gasifies, at a rate of about 0.1% to 0.2% of cargo per day. One strategy is to use this boil-off as fuel for the ship's propulsion. To do this and to provide electricity for all the process equipment onboard, the ship carries its own power plant. The vessel and all the processes aboard are controlled from a control room and connected with the command bridge where navigation happens. So far, this would be a sophisticated Automation system, based on DCS. But Digitalization lifts the operational performance further above this. Take the example of boil-off, which is essentially a loss of payload and should be reduced to the minimum. One factor limiting boil-off is temperature. But cooling the tanks also costs a lot of energy. The best strategy to manage this trade-off over the course of the cruise, is to already know which ambient temperature will be present at what part of the trip. Algorithms are then able to optimize. Another factor that provokes boil-off is sloshing of the LNG inside the tanks. When the vessel is going through heavy swell, negotiating high waves, the entire ship is rotating around its three axes. That makes the LNG swash around in the tanks. Imagine more than 250'000 m³ of liquid moving. This is a lot of kinetic energy and the propulsion system will have to partially compensate for these movements, which drives up fuel cost. But the sloshing can also accelerate the boil-off, leading to massive cargo loss. Marine advisory systems that take into account the properties of the vessel, measure the sloshing activity, utilize weather data, such as direction and strengths of wind, water currents, and wave profiles are able to adaptively calculate the best route, as well as tiny navigational counter-moves that keep the vessel on the water in a far more smooth and controlled manner. We can compare this to the ability of a waiter, to swiftly carry a very full glass of beer through a busy pub, careful to not bump into other people while not spilling any of the drink. Just imagine the waiter doing this in a storm with 20 meter high waves, and a glass that contains half a billion pints. Another factor that drives fuel savings is optimal trimming of the vessel. Trimming allows the captain to have the ship sit on the water in a straight fashion. If the vessel is too heavy at its stern, the bow will lift up and is hit by headwinds. Also the hulk is then not gliding through the water in the most efficient way. Similar issues occur if the bow is too low. A human captain has the experience to trim a ship by pumping ballast water between special tanks in the vessel's bowels so that it rests flush on the water. But in real conditions, with winds blowing from a certain direction and currents attacking the boat, perhaps from another direction, sitting flush on the water is not ideal. It is counter-intuitive. Sitting slightly skewed, however, can then be better. It is almost bizarre, but by pumping ballast water to different parts of the hulk, artificially intelligent advisory systems are able to actually bend the ship's body. Over the entire length of a 300m long vessel, this effect can be as much as a meter. While a human captain would never arrive at such a weird trim, the AI calculating the interventions of the autonomous trim system derives such a 'banana shape' as optimal in the vessel's real-world situation, reducing fuel consumption by several percent. Like in some of the other examples, the experience of a captain from hundreds of voyages can be augmented with an AI system, which applies machine learning from millions of simulated scenarios.

Future scenarios

Pervasive Robotization and the renewed focus on additive manufacturing, especially 3D printing, will allow mass customization of products. Big Data on the retail side of businesses makes it possible to predict better - how much and what the market will demand. Learning algorithms will adapt production cycles and effectively allow a single unit of a product to be made, just in time for its customer to request it. We call this 'lot size one.' In conventional manufacturing, lot sizes are a trade-off between actual, volatile demand for a standard catalog product and the economy of making large amounts in one batch. AI-supported predictive sales & production management helps to understand the demand better, while 3D printing and flexible Robotization allow customization without tool swapping or change over time. Once this offering is available to customers, both in B2B and B2C markets, off-the-shelf products will have a delicate position. In consumer businesses, we can observe this change for quite a while. You can order a birthday cake online, configure its decorations, and even upload the design or text you want to have on top. It is then 3D printed just in time for fresh delivery. Meal kit companies, such as Hello Fresh, offer customizable recipes, with precisely the amounts of ingredients needed to cook the meal for a defined number of people. Instead of buying a dozen packages of standard-sized components, leaving a lot of leftovers, this method allows cooking a perfect-sized meal without any waste. On the supply management side of this operation, big data allows maximization of economies of scale to an even higher degree than a food chain could achieve, which often wrongly predicts consolidated demand for goods. With almost no need for inventory, meal kit providers can drive capital turnover to very high numbers, maximizing return on capital in spite of narrow margins.

The more individualized consumption becomes, the more critical transport logistics will be. CO_2 neutral, autonomous transport with ground-based or airborne drones will be crucial. That brings us to the topic of mobility. Autonomous transport, mainly based on electric propulsion, is the future. Whether the electricity comes from batteries in smaller vehicles, fuel cells in medium to large vehicles, or renewable gas turbines, or even fusion, in heavy-duty vehicles, does not matter. With perhaps the exception of long haul aircraft, electricity will rule. For this, power networks need to become smart. Network optimization with wide area demand analytics and virtualization of distributed generation assets becomes a must. Fast-acting, market-based intervention, using AI-supported optimization, will make the best use of existing power resources.

There are two most essential roles Digitalization will play over the course of the next fifty years. First of all, it is to be the enabler for the next pivotal rounds in the other three Realms of Innovation. In Mechanization, this will be nanoengineering and 3D printing, while in the area of Energization it will be pervasive renewables and fusion. And in Automation, autonomous systems. To push these innovations over the finishing line, Digitalization, using big data and AI based on machine learning, will be fundamental.

The other essential role has to do with compensating for the ugly side effects that our technological progress has exposed. Industrialization started in a way that damaged the well-being of our civilization. And once Electrification allowed amplification of Industrialization with seemingly unlimited fossil fuel-based energy, it managed to endanger our entire planet. Robotization has helped us to start to slow down the human impact on nature, climate, and the Earth. The role of Informatization has always been to generate negentropy, as we discussed in chapter five. Negentropy holds the potential to counter entropy, while Automation can only slow entropy down. Societies and economies that manage to leverage this effect and democratize knowledge while furthering the development towards digitalized optimization, will win any race for competitiveness. The ability of an economy and its main actors to generate negentropy is correlated to their capability to avoid waste and nonproductive use of assets. During Industrialization, the race was about volume output. With Electrification, the winner was whoever connected the most economic actors to the power grid. During Robotization, everything was about lifting the productivity of labor and capital. The next battle is about negentropy. We are sure that countries that fall behind in this field or even become backward-oriented in some romanticized 'good old times' attitude will not only do harm to our civilization but will catapult themselves into a loser's spot in the global economic race.

Future scenarios

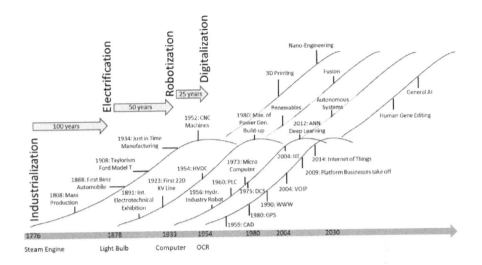

AI: Artificial Intelligence
ANN: Artificial Neural Network
CAD: Computer Aided Design
DCS: Distributed Control System
GPS: Global Positioning System
HVDC: High Voltage Direct Current

IIT: Industrial IT
OCR: Optical Character Recognition
PLC: Programmable Logic Controller
VOIP: Voice over IP
WWW: World Wide Web

We are using artificial intelligence successfully in narrow, defined areas, mainly making use of the ability of machine learning techniques to churn through massive data sets to learn how to react. The next step will be to broaden this approach by combining several different AI engines that are focused on specific problem fields and let them collaborate for adaptive behavior. Autonomous vehicles might be the first application for that. Whether we will ever be able to create a

247

general AI, a machine that possesses human intelligence, is still the question. And whether we should if we could.

Before that, we might see another revolution in the Realm of Informatization. This development started in 1971, just half a quarter-century after the start of Digitalization, when Paul Berg created the first recombinant strain of DNA by splicing and assembling DNA from the lambda virus and the SV40 monkey virus. DNA is one of the two information containers in organisms. The other one is memory. Informatization has allowed us to break the shackle of memory being restricted to our brain by expressing it through oracy and literacy. Genetic engineering is allowing us to do the same with DNA. And while this creates a lot of anxiety and fear, the ability to engineer the genome of a biological being is such a powerful tool that it will kick off the Third Evolution. The First Evolution is what created life on Earth. It happens through the intrinsic mechanism of life itself: recombination, mutation, and selection of genotype variants in a species. We humans brought to fruition the Second Evolution, which is not codified in the genetic code of our species, but in our social, innovation-oriented science and education. This Second Evolution needed intelligence to originate and the Realm of Informatization to manifest.

Future scenarios

Humankind uses the power of the Second Evolution to evolve much faster and far beyond the reach of the original First Evolution. Our scientific approach will allow us to soon alter the genetic code of our own species, which will again massively propel the evolution of our species forward.

Like perhaps never before in the history of our species, we will have to think ahead, to assess the meaning and potential threat of our innovation drive. The number of ethical questions around genetic self-engineering is daunting. But at the same time, we need to ask ourselves why we exist. Does life need us? Are we a deviation, a perversion of life? So far, we have created enormous devastation on our planet, have contributed to the extinction of many species, and have altered the climate to the degree that endangers countless habitats. If we try to look at this with a positive spin, we could say that nature, or life, is making an investment that costs for some time but will eventually yield a return. We have been on the planet as humankind for about one million years. Within the last two hundred years, the evolutionary cash flow we have brought to life on Earth was profoundly negative. What could the role of a highly intelligent, creative, self-evolving species on Earth be? There is only one purpose that justifies such a species. And that would be its ability to build an ark and take all of Earth's life to Earth 2. Maybe that is why we exist: as a safety measure for life. Like insurance, we could bring life to other planets to safeguard it from coincidental total extinction. The Fourth Evolution will begin with the first general AI-equipped artificial life form. If we ever have the opportunity to do this, one big question will certainly arise. What should be on the ark to Earth 2? Biological life or artificial life?

Or both?

Made in the USA
Middletown, DE
17 May 2021